WHITE STAR LINE

SUMMER TIME TABLE

Steamers Run Daily Except as Noted
Subject to Change Without Notice

TOLEDO AND DETROIT

GOING NORTH, READ DOWN		SUNDAYS	CENTRAL STANDARD TIME	Mls.	SUNDAYS	GOING SOUTH, READ UP	
In effect June 15 to Sept. 2	In effect April 20 to Oct. 5	Leave Toledo 9 15 AM / 2 30 PM / Arrive Sugar Is. / Arrive Detroit			Arrive Toledo 1 00 PM / 9 00 " / Arrive Sugar Is. / Leave Detroit	In effect April 20 to Oct. 5	In effect June 15 to Sept. 2
2 30 PM	°8 30 AM	12 00 M	Lv ...... TOLEDO, OHIO ...... Ar		8 30 AM	9 45 AM	1 00 PM
5 30 "	11 30 "	5 30 PM	Ar .... SUGAR ISLAND PARK Lv		5 50 "	6 30 PM	9 45 AM
5 55 "	11 35 "	Arrive	Lv .... SUGAR ISLAND PARK .... Ar	42	5 45 "	Leave	8 30 "
7 15 "	1 00 PM	Detroit 1 45 PM / 7 15 "	Ar ..... DETROIT, MICH. Lv	60	‡4 30 "	8 30 AM / 5 00 PM	

DETROIT AND PORT HURON

GOING NORTH, READ DOWN			CENTRAL STANDARD TIME	GOING SOUTH, READ UP		
In effect June 15 to Sept. 22	In effect April 13 to Oct. 1	In effect June 18 to Sept. 1		In effect June 18 to Sept. 1	In effect April 13 to Oct. 1	In effect June 15 to Sept. 22
§8 45 am	2 30 pm	† 4 00 pm	Lv ..... DETROIT, MICH. ..... Ar	‡8 40 am	11 30 am	8 50 pm
10 35 "	4 20 "	† 6 00 "	*Old Club	†6 50 "	9 45 "	7 10 "
10 41 "	4 26 "	† 6 05 "	*Hotel Muscamoot	†6 45 "		7 05 "
10 45 "	4 30 "	† 6 10 "	*Rushmere	†6 43 "	9 40 "	7 02 "
10 50 "	4 35 "	† 6 15 "	*STAR ISLAND	†6 40 "	9 35 "	7 00 "
10 56 "	4 40 "	† 6 20 "	*Marshland	†6 35 "	9 30 "	6 50 "
11 00 "	4 45 "	† 6 25 "	*Riverside	†6 30 "	9 28 "	6 45 "
11 05 "	4 50 "	† 6 30 "	*Forsters	†6 25 "		6 40 "
11 10 "	5 00 "	† 6 40 "	*Bedores	†6 20 "	9 25 "	6 37 "
11 20 "	5 10 "	† 7 00 "	*Muirs	†6 10 "	9 20 "	6 30 "
11 35 "	5 20 "	† 7 15 "	*TASHMOO PARK LANDING	†6 00 "	9 15 "	6 20 "
11 45 "	5 30 "	† 7 25 "	*Grande Pointe	†5 45 "	9 05 "	5 48 "
12 00 m	5 45 "	† 7 50 "	ALGONAC	†5 30 "	8 50 "	5 34 "
12 15 pm	6 00 "	† 8 10 "	*PORT LAMBTON, ONT.	†5 15 "	8 35 "	5 15 "
12 35 "	6 20 "	† 8 40 "	MARINE CITY	†5 00 "	8 20 "	4 58 "
1 10 "	7 05 "	† 9 30 "	ST. CLAIR		7 55 "	4 28 "
1 33 "	7 35 "		*Stag Island		7 30 "	4 09 "
1 51 "	8 00 "	†10 15 "	*South Park		7 15 "	3 54 "
2 10 "	8 05 "	†10 20 "	SARNIA, ONT.		7 05 "	3 39 "
2 15 "	8 15 "	†10 30 "	Ar .. PORT HURON, MICH. .. Lv	11 00 pm	‡7 00 "	3 30 "

*Flag Stations—Steamers stop on signal when time is given only
+Daily except Sundays
°Sundays, leave 9.15 a. m.
§Sunday morning steamers leave 9.00
‡Sundays, leave one-half hour later

Connections are made at TOLEDO with railroads diverging. At DETROIT with D. & C. magnificent steamers for Cleveland and Buffalo and all railroads. At SARNIA, Ont., with Northern Navigation Co. Steamers for Sault Ste. Marie, Port Arthur and Duluth and Grand Trunk Railway for all points in Canada. At PT. HURON with Pt. Huron and Duluth Steamers for Duluth.

Steamers Leave Foot of

Adams Street	Butler Street	Griswold Street
Toledo, Ohio	Port Huron, Mich.	Detroit, Mich.

B. W. PARKER, President and General Manager . . . Detroit
JOHN PRIDGEON, Vice-President . . . . Detroit
C. F. BIELMAN, Traffic Manager . . . . Detroit
GEO. E. PHILLIPS, Treasurer and Assistant Traffic Manager . . Detroit
E. H. AYER, T. P. A. and Exn. Agent . . . . Detroit
C. LEIDICH, Ticket Agent . . . . 174 Griswold St., Detroit
A. N. KNAPP, Agent . . . . . Toledo
H. E. STALKER, D. P. A. . . . . . Toledo
GEO. H. COURSE, Agent . . . . . Port Huron
NORTHERN NAV. CO., Agents . . . . Sarnia, Ont.
F. B. CLARKE, Agent . . . . . London, Ont.

WHEN DETROIT RODE THE WAVES

SPECIAL

COLLECTOR EDITION

72/200

WHEN DETROIT RODE THE WAVES

THE WAVES

A summer cruise along the Detroit and St. Clair rivers
aboard the riverboats of the early 20th century

by
MICHAEL M. DIXON

Featuring
ILLUSTRATIONS FROM ORIGINAL PERIOD POST CARDS
and a brief
HISTORY OF POST CARDS IN AMERICA

MERVUE PUBLICATIONS

ABOUT THE AUTHOR:

MICHAEL M. DIXON is a descendant of early settlers who played active roles in Detroit's transformation from "Furs to Factories." Many of these same people were pioneers in the transformation of the St. Clair River Delta (the Flats) from isolated wetlands into one of the nation's most desirable summer retreats. Michael has always had a strong affection for the Flats and has detailed its history in his book "Life at the Flats – The Golden Era of the St. Clair River Delta." In this volume he retraces the South Channel of the St. Clair River and continues north to Port Huron and south to Toledo.

Michael is a commercial banking officer in metro Detroit. In the summer he enjoys sailing Lake St. Clair and in the winter he spends his vacations leading small groups on cultural tours of Mexico. He is working on his next book, "Motormen and Yachts," a history of Gray Marine Motor Company and the tale of the marine engine in the development of the early automobile industry.

For additional information on obtaining copies of his books or joining one of his tours look at his web page: www.go.to/mikesworld. He may be contacted by writing to him at 321 Moross, Grosse Pointe Farms, MI 48236 or by e-mail to mikesworld@go.to or moross321@aol.com.

COVER: Cover design is from an original painting by Detroit area artist Nancy Pitel. An award winning artist and published photographer, her work ranges from portrait painting, wall murals and illustrating childrens' books to wedding, news and fine art photography. Her business, Angel Baby Portraits, works with hospital bereavement groups, creating painted portraits of still-born babies that facilitate families' grieving process. She may be reached at 248-288-8278 or npitel@aol.com.

Limited Editions:
Patrons' Special Collector Edition, 100
Special Collector Edition, 200

EAN ISBN: 0-9710833-0-4

LIBRARY OF CONGRESS CONTROL NUMBER: 2001126612

PATRONS' DEDICATION

Publishing of *When Detroit Rode the Waves* could not have been possible without the confidence and financial support of the Prepublishing Subscribers. Every single one was appreciated. A special thank you is dedicated to the following Patrons:

Mr. And Mrs. Antoine Abi Raji
The Abrams Family
James A. Anderson
Sheridan and Judith Anderson
Michael & Catherine Badalamente
Dr. and Mrs. Thomas W. Baumgarten
Nancy Besemer
Mr. John L.Booth, II
Chuck and Scotty Brockman
    and SOS Channel Lights
Paul J. Chauvin
Roger & Lynn Christel
Mary Hubbard Livingstone Clark
    and David Sanders Clark
Laura Murphy Creamer
George and Barbara Crown
    and The Waterfront Shop
Edward B. Dennert
James and Mary Ann Devereaux
Joan Mulford Dixon
Russell & Susan Dixon
Mary and Gregg McDuffee
James E. Eason
David M. & Nelli Elle
Norman C. Engel
Mr. & Mrs. Charles T. Fisher III
Mr. And Mrs. Douglas R. Fox
Friends of the Harsen's Island
    Preservation Association
David & Shelley Gagnon
Nancy P. Gard
Roger and Joanna Garrett
Mr. and Mrs. George Gill
Bruce, Katherine and
    Geoffrey Greening
Gary and Ann Grout
Rebekah E. Gutierrez
Helga and Friedrich
    Hachenberg, Minden, Germany

Robert Hafel
Rachael Harla
Mr. And Mrs. Lawrence Havens
William & Lois Henning
J. J. and Laura Nike
Gerald and Virginia Hindman
Bob and Natalie Hindman
Mrs. George Hudson III
Jim and Nina Johnson
Ralph W. Kandt
Mark and Lori Kosanke
Rev. Sig Kowalczyk
In memory of Ben and Eoula Lindquist,
    who met on the Tashmoo
Thomas and Susan Mulford Little
Tom & Annie Lockwood
Helen Marttila, Wixom, Mi.
McGuires Fine Art-Northville
Kenneth & Anita McIntyre
Patrick M. McQueen
Peter W. Meek
Ronald D. Moore
James and Jean Nelson
Larry and Karen Ortel
John and Phyllis Osler
Rose and Howard Rasch, Blmfield Hills, Mi.
Dr. and Mrs. W. Ryniewicz & Family
Shawn A. Santo, Pure Detroit
Jack and Barbara Schramm
Kenneth E. Schramm
Mike and Sandy Skinner
Jim Stevenson
Stoneback and Family
Rev. Fr. Douglas J. Terrien KHS
Geo. A. Tinnerman, III
Henry C. Tinnerman
Jean and Richard Weber
A. Lee & Nancy E. Wright
Ed and Sue Young of Eastpointe, Mi.

PREFACE

In 1987, in the Preface of my second volume on the history of the St. Clair Flats, I made the following statement:

"The most perplexing problem has been addressing the question, 'When do you stop writing about the history of a community?' Certainly there is more to tell. Everyone has a story that is important to them. After many interviews, reading everything I could uncover and looking at the photographs of everyone willing to show their collection, I arbitrarily said, 'enough.' The reader will have to determine if I was correct."

Since that time there was a volume III and in 1999 I wrote in the preface to the Collector's Edition:

"The original volumes have now been long out of print and interest in a reprinting has continued. This Collector's Edition is an edited collection of material from the original three volumes. I sincerely hope that the following pages continue to bring pleasure to those who love the Flats of the St. Clair River Delta."

Encouraged by the positive reception of the earlier books, this current volume is a natural extension. The ships that passed the Flats also connected Toledo and Port Huron and in many cases post cards were the best or only printed images remaining for some long gone scenes. As a result I was led to study the history of the excursion steamers and the post card publishers. Both were experiencing the peak in their popularity during the early 1900's. Reading a number of the annual publications of the White Star Line inspired me to recreate the route and tell the story of the excursion ships and post cards.

Many people assisted in making it possible to publish this series. Most have been acknowledged before but, special thanks must be offered to the following whose assistance and support made this possible. All efforts to organize and expand the content of family memorabilia would have resulted in merely a nice scrapbook if, it had not been for the generous assistance provided by Jim Babcock, Frank Sladden, and Nick and Joan Sarzinski. They displayed the first draft and personally promoted the preprinting sales. The late Jeremy John insisted on providing professional typesetting and keylining and Marty Hair provided diligent proof reading of the first volumes, both of whom certainly broadened the appeal of the final printing.

Many made it possible to expand the material from a family scrapbook to a substantial collection of memorabilia. My thanks again go out to all. To single out a few, the staffs of the Burton Historical Collection of the Detroit Public Library, Dossin Great Lakes Museum and the Henry Ford Museum & Greenfield Village, the late Algonac historian, Betty Droulard, the late Tashmoo historian, J. Michael O'Brien.

For this volume, special thanks for assistance again goes to Jack Schramm for advice and sharing his extensive post card collection. The late Gordon Bugbee generously shared his knowledge of steamship history with all and was looking forward to editing the content of this publication. Cynthia Read-Miller has given me encouragement, technical advice and, provided valuable time to proof read the draft, contributing much to make this text readable. Years ago the late Susan Glass shared with me her copy of the White Star Line Magazine from which the cruise description originated. Thanks to George and Barbara Crown/The Waterfront Shop and Chuck Brockman/SosChannel Lights whose selfless promotion of pre-publishing sales especially pleased the printer's accountant. Finally, it was the considerable time and effort provided by J.J. Hile who shared his extensive post card collection and worked closely with me to locate additional cards.

To each and everyone of you, I am sincerely grateful.

Michael M. Dixon
April, 2001

FOREWORD

The old adage holds true for Michael M. Dixon's books, "A picture is worth a thousand words." In his previous books on Harsen's Island and the St. Clair Flats he has skillfully used photographs, maps and other graphics to bring to life this summer resort.

His new book takes us a step further in the history of the region. It is a journey along the waterfront from Toledo to Port Huron fittingly illustrated with post cards from the early 20th century. At the same time that picture post cards became a popular addition to American life, Detroit riverboat travel experienced its golden years. Interestingly, also at this time the Detroit Publishing Company was arguably the most important American color post card printer. That is why this book is illustrated with many Detroit Publishing Company post cards. By combining a history of post cards in America with a summer cruise along the Detroit and St. Clair rivers the author provides not only a captivating story, but also a unique mind's eye journey in his book, *When Detroit Rode the Waves*.

This book not only helps us understand the history of post cards, it opens a fascinating window on yesterday. The section on the Detroit Publishing Company* covers important detail regarding the company's founding, business practices and production of so many colorful post cards. Linking the post cards from almost 100 years ago to the map of the locations they depict and reprinting the text of the White Star Magazine of 1906 provides texture for imagining the experience of water travel during its prime. Travelers from the beginning of the 20th century bought the post cards for souvenirs so they could remember their summer trips along the shores of Lake St. Clair.

One of my favorite recreational drives is along Jefferson Avenue from Detroit to Port Huron. At times I have gazed across Lake St. Clair and the Detroit and St. Clair rivers and wondered what it was like to travel in this region before the automobile. In this book, Michael Dixon provides the opportunity to take a journey back through time almost 100 years ago. It is a journey along the water that shows through post cards how the waterfront appeared to the riverboat traveler. It is a journey that our imaginations can take today because of this wonderful book.

Cynthia Read-Miller
Senior Curator, Photography and Prints
Henry Ford Museum & Greenfield Village

The Detroit Publishing Company collection of Henry Ford Museum & Greenfield Village consists of over 30,000 vintage photographic prints, 5,000 color and sepia lithograph prints and 15,000 post cards.

TABLE OF CONTENTS

INTRODUCTION

On New Year's Eve 2000, Mayor Dennis Archer broke the seal on the box that Mayor William C. Maybury had closed on December 31, 1900. An excerpt from Mayor Maybury's letter:

.....We are well aware that the century closing has been marvelous in its achievements and we might be fairly excused for believing that the limit of possibilities has been accomplished in many ways, but on the contrary we do not so believe because the past has taught us that what seemed to be impossible has been already accomplished, and we would therefore not be greatly surprised at greater accomplishments in the future.

We communicate by telegraph and telephone over distances that at the opening of the nineteenth century were insurmountable. We travel at a rate not dreamed of then. The powers of electricity have been applied marvelously, and compressed air and other agencies are now undergoing promising experiments. We travel by railroad and steam power from Detroit to Chicago in less than eight hours, and to New York City by several routes in less than twenty hours. How much faster are you travelling? How much farther have you annihilated time and space and what agencies are you employing to which we are strangers? We talk by long distance telephone to the remotest cities in our own country, and with a fair degree of practical success. Are you talking with foreign lands and to the islands of the sea by the same method? .....

Respectfully and affectionately submitted,

William C. Maybury, Mayor.
(Detroit, Mich., Dec. 31, 1900)

At the dawn of the 20th century, Detroit's slogan was justifiably, *In Detroit-Life is Worth Living.* Opportunities abounded and the people came, it was "*a great time to be in Detroit.*"[1]

The 1906 White Star Line yearbook described Detroit as one of the most unique and remarkable cities in America and went on to say, "*Take it all in all, Detroit is the most beautiful city in the American continent. Here Art and Nature vie with each other in providing beautiful effects. It is laid out in such a way that the center cannot shift, its broad avenues converging to one point. The land rises gradually from the riverbank giving perfect drainage, and many streets have from two to four rows of shade trees. There are big and little parks scattered north, east and west, and a great broad boulevard, fourteen miles on and two hundred feet wide, encircles the entire city... the center of the city is after a plan adopted at Washington, and still earlier at Versailles, France.*"[2] The city's commanding position on the chain of lakes, together with good arable land and natural resources combined to attract settlers, farmers, merchants, manufacturers, investors and pleasure seekers in ever increasing numbers.

By 1906 the city had some of the greatest industrial establishments in the world. Aside from the specialties in which it was beyond competition, the city was remarkable for the variety of its products. Its leading industry was the manufacturing of cars, rail cars, or if taken in aggregate, the chemical industry. Following is the value of production of the leading industries in 1906 dollars, as provided by the Chamber of Commerce:

```
Chemicals ............................................................ $30,900,000
        Druggists' preparations ............................... 10,900,000
        Paints and varnish ...................................... 10,000,000
        Coarse chemicals ....................................... 10,000,000
Car building, freight, passenger and electric ............... 25,000,000
Food products, including slaughtering and meat packing ............ 15,000,000
Automobiles .............................................................. 12,000,000
Clothing, knit goods, boots and shoes, etc. ............... 10,500,000
Newspapers and other printing and publishing ........... 10,200,000
Stove and steam heating apparatus .............................. 9,300,000
Foundry and machine shop products ............................. 9,500,000
Furniture .................................................................... 5,500,000
Tobacco and cigars ...................................................... 4,500,000
Malt liquors ................................................................ 3,600,000
```

Thirty-five industries produced over $1,000,000 each in 1906. More than 80% of all the computing machines manufactured in the country were produced in Detroit, along with more commercial steamships than any other freshwater port and it was undoubtedly the greatest pleasure-boat building center of the continent. Fifteen hundred factories gave employment to 100,000 mechanics, clerks and laborers. Detroit was already known as the Motor City owing to its leading development of internal combustion engines, first for industrial, agricultural and pleasure boating applications.[3]

From the city's many docks, hardworking Detroiters could board any number of passenger ships in the nation's largest fleet. Either a short cruise or a long distance cruise, for necessary transportation or merely for pleasure, were readily available at affordable prices. Island parks served by Detroit's passenger steamers were as close as Belle Island. Within a few hours travel in either direction the choices multiplied: Tashmoo Park on Harsen's Island, Camp Algonac on Russell Island and Stag Island to the north; Bob-Lo and Sugar Island on the Detroit River and Put-in-Bay and Cedar Point to the south, in Lake Erie were all popular destinations. In 1904, Detroit steamers carried over seven million passengers to various destinations. That exceeded the number carried from all other U.S. Great Lakes ports combined. This remained the case until the last years of the Bob-Lo boats.

14

It has been 10 years since the last cruise was available on any of the era's original excursion steamers.[4] Little can be done to truly recreate the thrill of the ride or the excitement of the destinations, but following is the story of the fleet and a recreation of a cruise from Toledo to Port Huron.

This same period of industrial and recreational opportunities was also the time that the U.S. government authorized the one cent "Private Mailing Card" in 1898, the "Post Card," in 1901, and first permitted writing on a divided back in 1907. When combined with the new photographic and color printing technologies, post card collecting quickly became a national pass-time and one of the most important collectible hobbies in the world. Detroit publishers were among the leaders in the business. Arguably the leading post card publisher of the time was the Detroit Publishing Company. Since 1897 they had been amassing a huge collection of negatives of scenic places and impressive things from around the country. Following is its story and many of its local river-view post cards are reproduced.

The complete descriptive text of the White Star Line's 1906 yearbook is reproduced in the following pages. To borrow from it again, "With these few remarks by way of introduction, the reader is earnestly requested to read the following pages, to the end, that he may become familiar with at least some of the interesting objects to be seen in a day's outing..."

---

1. Detroit's official slogan in the year 2000 was, "It's a great time in Detroit."

2. After a disastrous fire destroyed the city in 1805, the U.S. Congress authorized the Governor and three Supreme Judges to rebuild the city according to their best judgement. The chief justice, Augustus B. Woodward, had spent some time in Washington and had become enamored of the plan of that city as first conceived by the eminent French architect, Pierre L'Enfant.

3. The practical applications in industry, agriculture and pleasure boating gave cause to the development of the internal combustion engine. Oats and public transportation were cheap and roads were to bad to have been much encouragement to the birth of the personal transportation machine. But the prosperity of the area and the great recreational waterfront destinations available gave residents the wealth and motivation to acquire lightweight mobile power plants. Even if the early one cylinder engines did misfire and stall, the momentum kept the craft gliding through the water. But on land, with even the slightest upgrade, a backfire would bring the vehicle to a stop. The driving technology for the automobile was developed on the river.

4. At the time of writing this, there is still optimism that one of the Bob-Lo Steamers can again be commissioned for summer excursions.

And still the crowds come and come. Is there no end to them? Has the whole population of Detroit chosen this special day to go to the Flats? No, this is only a fair sample of every Sunday morning in summer; this is the Sunday crowd . . ."
Detroit News Tribune, "Michigan's Venice," August 18, 1895.

DETROIT'S PASSENGER RIVERBOAT SERVICE

Prior to the 1899 launching of the Steamer TASHMOO and the consolidation of the White Star Line, many companies competed fiercely to dominate the passenger business along Detroit's waterways. Following, their stories are briefly told.

The Formative Years (1830-1885)

The primitive ARGO*, launched in October 1829, was Detroit's first steamboat. A more conventional steamer, GENERAL GRATIOT, began service in 1831 with one round-trip weekly to each Toledo, Monroe and Port Huron. For the next 20 years its Capt. Edwards had a hand in establishing all the passenger services radiating from Detroit, including all points between Port Huron and Buffalo.

In 1836 the steamer ERIE began competing, but it was in 1840 when Capt. Samuel Ward** and his nephew Eber Brock Ward, of Marine City, launched the HURON that the competition for passenger really began. That is when the Ward steamboat empire began its expansion to over 20 ships in a dozen years and serving all the middle lakes and Lake Superior.

After E. B. Ward died in 1875***, Robert L. Montgomery continued to manage the local service as the Star Line. The EVENING STAR was being paired with the MILTON D. WARD, running on alternate days between days between Detroit and Port Austin on Lake Huron. About 1875 the SAGINAW joined the WARD on Lake Huron so that the STAR could make the Detroit-Port Huron round trip daily. About the same time, Montgomery joined Wm. E. Warriner to open the 3-story Star Island House, the first public hotel at the St. Clair Flats, on the south channel of the St. Clair River. This was to attract excursionists not interested in the full day trip. The restaurant of this hotel was able to receive Star Line passengers for fish and frog suppers, a great boon to promoting

*A platform and a 4-hp steam engine straddled two 55-foot white pine logs.
**Capt. Ward was the first to bring a ship through the Erie Canal.
***Since the 1850s his investments had diversified to include lumber, railroads, the nation's first Bessemer steel plant and the Great Lakes' first iron shipyard, in Wyandotte. When he died at age 63 he was by far Michigan's wealthiest citizen.

excursion business as a compliment to the transportation business. Capable of serving 500 at one sitting, it could claim to have the largest dinning room in the state.

In the early eighties Messrs. Newberry and McMillan, investors in the Detroit and Cleveland Line (D&C Line) of night boats, took control of the Star Line. They did this to make a link running steamers all the way from Cleveland to the Straits of Mackinac, where they were building an Upper Peninsula railroad. D&C steamers soon took over the Lake Huron routes, but the Star Line benefited by establishing daily steamer service between Detroit and Toledo. (This route had been monopolized by the railroads since the ARROW withdrew in 1858.)

Transitional Years (1886 – 1898)

1886 brought a turbulent fight for river passengers with the shipping interests of Darius Cole and Stephen Grummond joining forces to rival the river monopoly of the Star Line. The challenge began with the lines competing on the basis of speed, quickly followed by fare cutting. This reached its peak on May 13 when both lines carried passengers free of charge. By the end of May they both retreated and asked a twenty-five cent fare which advanced to fifty cents by mid-season. However, for the rest of the season the Star Line barred the others from stopping at the Star Island House. Capt. Grummond had property nearby and arranged to dock the old sidewheeler KEWEENAW into a canal and promoted the merits of Keweenaw Island's summer hotel. In July, 1888, Capt. Cole and W. K. Muir, a Star Line director, joined forces to buy the Star Line. All other Star Line directors resigned except for Captain Grummond. When Cole won control, he hired Charles F. Bielman, to be the manager.

In 1894 a syndicate headed by Aaron A. Parker and Captain James Millen peacefully gained control of the awkward alliance of the Star-Cole-Red & White Star Lines. Bielman continued as manager. Indeed, Bielman was forming his own shipping dynasty. Newly prosperous as the Star Line manager, in 1890 he married Kate Barlum, the daughter of a wealthy Detroit merchant. When he died in 1920, his role as manager went to his son, Charles F. Bielman, Jr. and in the mid-twenties his brother-in-law, John J. Barlum, became the president of the White Star Line and its successor the White Star Navigation Company.

For 1896, the Detroit, Belle Isle & Windsor Ferry Company (see page 39 for a brief history) became a player on the St. Clair River. The previous August the streetcar company stopped carrying passengers down to the docks, encouraging Belle Isle picnickers to take a trolley there instead. So, for 1896 the Ferry

Company made arrangements for a picnic ground off the South Channel of the St. Clair River. Bielman quickly arranged for a Star Line picnic ground. By July the Ferry Company withdrew from the St. Clair River competition. In 1897 the Ferry Co. purchased 10 acres on Bois Blanc (Bob-Lo) Island, made improvements and began taking excursionists there on June 1898.

For 1897 Bielman had arranged for the Star Line to acquire Tashmoo Park, a simple picnic ground on Harsen's Island. Immediate improvements included a dance hall and pavilions along with boats and fishing tackle to rent.

Tashmoo Park was also a strategic venture. The alliance with the Star-Cole group would be up in 1900 and the White Star steamers could again be kept from landing at the Star Island House. However, by this time day excursionists were demonstrating a preference for amusement parks and the White Star Line was preparing to cater to that crowd.

The White Star Line's Golden Era (1899 – 1911)

In 1899 the Parker-Millen interests consolidated their holdings into one big White Star Line. They determined to prevent another challenge to their dominance by building the long-promised 300-foot steamer for the Detroit-Port Huron, St. Clair Flats route. What became the Tashmoo was the masterpiece of the era's most prolific naval architect, Frank E. Kirby. At 303-feet and elegantly outfitted, the Tashmoo was foremost among the nation's excursion steamers. Besides broad decks for excursionists who would get off along the way, she had fine appointments for her passengers making connections in Port Huron and Sarnia. One of the most memorable features of the Tashmoo was the plate-glass windows, so numerous and low that the passengers in the grand salon, dining room or private parlors could enjoy the scenery equally with those outside.

The Tashmoo was launched on the next-to-the-last day of the "Gay Nineties." After completing the interior and other outfitting details she made her maiden voyage on June 9, 1900. However, even when brand new, Tashmoo's debut was already a lost race against obsolescence. She first reached Port Huron only weeks before interurban cars brought their first passengers from Detroit. Over the next year interurban cars also linked Detroit with Toledo. The steamers were no longer the only public transportation between the principal river towns. The river steamers had become only a pleasant alternative. The St. Clair Flats resorts continued to be an exception as the Flats road was still decades away.

Nevertheless, in 1901 the White Star Line commissioned the 276-foot steel hull Greyhound for that route. She was launched on February 16, 1902, and took her maiden voyage on June 5th. (Weeks later, on July 8th, the Columbia took her maiden voyage to Bob-Lo Island.)

In 1903 the Tashmoo closed the season boasting of having carried 224,162 passengers out of Detroit, a 22% increase over 1902. This was more than two-thirds of Detroit's 1900 population of 317,591.

In 1904 Detroit steamers carried over seven million passengers to various destinations. That exceeded the number carried from all other United States Great Lakes ports combined. This remained the case until the last years of the Bob-Lo boats.

By 1905 the White Star Line had its most complete array of offerings. That year the line acquired Sugar Island in the lower Detroit River from the Clark estate. (John P. Clark bought the island in 1851. As early as 1876 Clark's steamer RIVERSIDE had been taking picnickers there on its run to Wyandotte and Grosse Isle. Clark is also remembered for donating the Clark Park property to the City of Detroit.) Improvements to the island park provided a convenient excursion from Toledo and as a stop for excursionists traveling between Detroit and Toledo.

Years of Social and Technological Change (1912 – 1935)

People enamored with their new cars were going to dining and entertainment places their cars could reach. In 1912 the Detroit and Cleveland Line placed the first of Lake Erie's four "world's largest side-wheelers," City of Detroit III, on its Buffalo run. These were specifically designed to accommodate automobiles. Motorists could take their cars aboard and avoid much driving on poor roads. They could travel in comfort overnight and in the morning they would be miles farther away on their trip. That October the White Star Line's excursion manager noted that summer hotels in the Flats were losing patronage.

By the 1920's the automobile had practically eliminated excursion steamship business. The clubs, hotels and parks along the rivers suffered an irreversible decline in clientele and cottagers found themselves increasingly isolated. In 1921 a muddy seasonal road began to extend down the southeast shore of Harsen's Island. Improved and extended in stages, by 1938 a reliable road was completed extending all the way down the south channel.

In 1925, just when the Detroit and Cleveland Line was adding Lake Erie's biggest pair of night boats ever, the White Star Line corporation was dissolved. The rides at Sugar Island were moved to Tashmoo Park and the TASHMOO was the only steamer retained by the new White Star Navigation Company.

In the Wake of the Tashmoo (1936 -   )

The Tashmoo was far from her Port Huron route on the night of June 18, 1936, when she was irreparably damaged. She was downriver running a charter moonlight trip for 1500 members and friends of the Pals Social Club from Hamtramck. After leaving Sugar Island, she ripped her hull on an underwater obstruction. With the band playing the passengers were unaware of her plight until they were put ashore at Amherstburg, Ontario. A bus ride took them back home as the Tashmoo settled in eighteen feet of water. Her keel was irreparably broken and she was deemed a total loss.* The next year fittings were auctioned and her steel hull was scrapped at Sandwich, Ontario.

Charles F. Bielman, Jr., head of the successor Tashmoo Transit Company, talked of replacing the lost steamer, with a Lake Michigan excursion ship that was never identified. Unfortunately, at that time the Depression was at its worst. The D&C flagship night boats Greater Detroit and Greater Buffalo, spent the 1936 season laid up. The D&C Line also curtailed its regular service to Chicago and Mackinac Island and only maintained regular night runs to Cleveland and Buffalo on its smaller ships. None of Detroit's remaining day boats attempted to replace the Tashmoo on the regular river route, so only cruise ship passengers saw the St. Clair River scenery for the remainder of that season.

*The final blow to the Tashmoo did not take place until 1951. Since the Tashmoo was so beloved by thousands of excursionists, the dismantled parts were sold at auction. The pilothouse and a large portion of the deck immediately below were purchased by Captain J. A. McKenty, a tugboat captain from Chatham, Ontario.

Captain McKenty turned the cabin into a summer cottage. For many years the "Tashmoo Cottage" was a Chatham area tourist attraction, a chance to view the Tashmoo one more time. Unfortunately, on June 10, 1951, the surviving Tashmoo was destroyed by fire.

Largely due to the efforts of the late Tashmoo historian J. Michael O'Brien, in May, 1985, the Tashmoo was inducted into the National Maritime Hall of Fame at the U.S. Merchant Marine Academy in King's Point, N. Y.

In 1937 the newly formed Detroit-St. Clair Navigation Co. ran the City of Hancock, but at one-third the length of the Tashmoo she hardly inspired a revival of day cruises. After a year or two she went to Lake Erie.

In 1938 the D&C Line began making regular Sunday and holiday excursions from Detroit up into Lake Huron and return. That same year the Detroit-Windsor Ferry Company sold its interurban franchise* to the Tunnel Company and its flagship, the steamer Columbia began making Sunday and holiday excursions to Port Huron. Notably, the Columbia was purely an excursion boat, and offered more shaded open deck space than either the Tashmoo or the D&C boats. Even if the public rooms weren't as impressive, she had the better ballroom. These trips became especially profitable during the war years when gas rationing kept automobiles at home.

In the late 1940's the St. Clair River route belonged to the Ashley & Dustin Line's Put-In-Bay. For several years she made daily afternoon trips to Tashmoo Park with some weekend trips on to Port Huron. In 1951 the D&C Line and Tashmoo Park both closed for good. Finally, in 1953 the Put-In-Bay was sold and that October the superstructure was burned in the middle of Lake St. Clair to facilitate scrapping the iron hull.

Between 1957 and 1962 the Aquarama made Friday excursions to Port Huron. At 520 feet she was by far the longest day steamer ever on the river. She had three dance floors and six restaurants and bars and broad sundecks extending much of her length topside. However, her viability depended on the new St. Lawrence Seaway letting her out of the Great Lakes in wintertime to run similar day service between Miami and Havana. Castro's revolution thwarted that, and after 1962 she sat idle.

The Bob-Lo boats, Columbia and Ste. Clair, continued to give Detroiters the opportunity to experience the pleasure of riverboat travel. They provided regularly scheduled cruises to Bob-Lo Island, moonlight cruises and occasional excursions as far as Port Huron until they were laid up at the end of the regular season in 1991. As of the writing of this chapter there is still optimism that one of the boats will be restored to working condition (see the Epilogue). But for now the age of grand riverboats in the Detroit area is only a memory.

*The ferry service begun by Hiram Walker in 1880, Walkerville and Detroit Ferry Company, continued to provide regular service from Detroit (foot of Jos. Campau) to Walkerville until May 15, 1942.

The last passenger ship to serve the Detroit-Port Huron route on a regular schedule was the Frank E. Kirby designed PUT-IN-BAY. Built in 1911, for the Ashley & Dustin Co., she first served the Detroit-Toledo route. After the TASHMOO was decommissioned in 1936, the PUT-IN-BAY began serving the Detroit-Port Huron run. At the close of the regular season in 1951 Tashmoo Park closed its doors for good. Viable support for passenger service on the St. Clair River was history and on October 3, 1953, the PUT-IN-BAY was set ablaze in Lake St. Clair, as a public service and as the best means of disposing of her superstructure before sending the hull to be scrapped at River Rouge. (Photo courtesy of the Dossin Great Lakes Museum)

FRANK E. KIRBY
Remembered

Frank E. Kirby was the nation's most prolific naval architect from the late 1800s through the mid 1920s. The "masterpiece for which he may be most remembered was the design of the Steamer TASHMOO, the flagship of the White Star Line. On the merits of her deign, Kirby won commissions with J. W. Millard for designing the largest day steamers in the country for the Hudson River Line. Before the TASHMOO Kirby was known to the general public for the Ashley & Dustin Co. excursion steamer FRANK E. KIRBY of 1890. However, for 46 years Kirby designed all of the Detroit and Cleveland Navigation Company (D&C) and Cleveland and Buffalo Transit Company (C&B) passenger steamers. As the consumate naval architect he was best known for five of their Lake Erie night boats, four of which claimed to be the largest sidewheelers in the world when they were launched.

The 472-foot CITY OF DETROIT III of 1912 was the most elegant of all lake steamers. Its Rococo Gothic smoking room survives today modified as the foyer to Detroit's Dossin Great Lakes Museum on Belle Isle. His largest were the 536-foor sisters built in 1924, GREATER DETROIT and GREATER BUFFALO.

But ships are ephemeral and of his fine passenger steamers, only the "Bob-Lo Boats" COLUMBIA and STE. CLAIR, survive in anything like their original appearance. All the other great ships were broken ups and scrapped by the end of the 1950s.

GUIDE TO DETROIT'S BOAT LINES AND LANDINGS

Reprinted from an information booklet distributed by the Wayne Hotel in 1908.

ALGOMA CENTRAL STEAMSHIP LINE – (Dock at the foot of First St.) Operating two steamships between Sandusky, Toledo, Detroit and way ports on the Georgian Bay route to Sault Ste. Marie and Mackinac. Fares, round trip, Detroit and Soo, $28.00. Detroit to the Soo, one way, $10.00, meals and berth included.

ANCHOR LINE – (Dock at the foot of First St.) Operating a line of palatial passenger and large freight steamers between Buffalo on the east and Duluth on the northwest. Stopping at Erie, Cleveland, Detroit, Port Huron, the "Soo," Marquette and Houghton. The star boats of the fleet are the Tionesta and Juanita.

ASHLEY AND DUSTIN LINE – (Dock at the foot of First St.) Operating the fast steamer Frank E. Kirby, a round trip daily to Put-in-Bay Island and Sandusky, 125 mile ride on Detroit River and Lake Erie, consuming 12 1/2 hours. Put-in-Bay is the island that Commodore Perry put into with his men after his great naval fight with the British in 1813. Fare 50 cents for the round trip.

DETROIT AND BUFFALO STEAMBOAT COMPANY – (Dock at the foot of Shelby) Entrance from Wayne Street. Operating daily boats between Detroit and Buffalo. The famous Eastern and Western States leaving either city late in the afternoon and reaching the other city early the following morning. Fare $3.50 one way. Special rates on weekend excursions. Distance about 285 miles.

DETROIT AND CLEVELAND NAVIGATION COMPANY – (Dock at the foot of Wayne Street) Operating nightly service between Detroit and Cleveland, departing from either city at 10:30 p.m. reaching the other at 6:00 a.m. The pride of the fleet is the new steamer City of Cleveland, built at a cost of $125,000, and known as the finest passenger ship afloat, even surpassing the famous "Sound Line" boats of the east. During July and August the line runs a daily boat between the two cities Tuesdays, Thursdays and Saturdays. Fare to Cleveland $2.00. Day trips $1.10. Weekend excursions Saturday, both ways, one fare for round trip.

TOLEDO AND MACKINAW DIVISIONS – (Dock at the foot of Wayne St.) Four boats a week between Toledo and St. Ignace, with stops at way ports and express passenger service June 25th to September 10th, from Detroit only. 410 miles from Toledo to St. Ignace, 60 miles from Detroit to Toledo.

BAY CITY DIVISION – (Dock at the foot of Randolph St.) Two boats a week between Detroit and Bay City. 229 miles. Time consumed about 21 hours.

NORTHERN STEAMSHIP COMPANY – (Dock at the foot of Cass) Operating the magnificent steamships Northwest and Northland, between Buffalo on the east, and Duluth and Chicago on the north and west. These boats are exclusively passenger ships, the largest of their type on the lakes, and stopping only at Cleveland, Detroit, Mackinac Island on both trips; the Duluth ship at the Soo, Marquette, Houghton and Hancock and the Chicago bound ship at Harbor Springs and Milwaukee. Distance, Detroit to Duluth, 808 miles, fare $25.00: Detroit to Chicago, 676 miles, $20.00.

NORTHERN NAVIGATION COMPANY – (Dock at Windsor, Grand Trunk Dock) Operating lines of steamers between Detroit and Duluth and the northern Lake Superior ports, Port Arthur or Fort William. Fare to Duluth, $20.75, to Port Arthur or Fort William, $18.25. Also operate a line of steamers making the Georgian Bay and Soo trip, but starting only from Sarnia, opposite Port Huron, on the Canadian side of the St. Clair River. For fares, see folders.

STAR-COLE LINE – (Dock at the foot of Randolph Street) Operating the steamer Huron between Cleveland, Toledo, Detroit, Port Huron and the Georgian Bay points. One round trip per week. Stopping at Goderich, Kincardine and way ports on the north and east of Georgian Bay. Fare, Detroit to Sault Ste. Marie, $13.00.

WHITE STAR LINE – (Dock at the foot of Griswold Street) Operating a fleet of passenger steamers to the Flats, "the Venice of America" and double daily service between Detroit and Port Huron with a single daily service to Toledo. Distance, Detroit to Port Huron, 65 miles, fare one way, 75 cents: to the Flats, (Star Island House) 25 miles, fare round trip, 75 cents. Distance to Toledo, 60 miles, fare, 75 cents.

SHOWCASE OF DETROIT'S PASSENGER RIVERBOATS

In addition to the TASHMOO, left and featured elsewhere, Detroit was the home port to numerous passenger riverboats during the years *When Detroit Rode the Waves.*

The DARIUS COLE, pictured in this 1891 advertisement, had a 215-foot iron hull built at Cleveland in 1885 specifically for the Detroit-Port Huron route.

29

GREYHOUND — the early GREYHOUND had originally been built for the D&C Line's lake routes and named NORTH WEST. In 1886, the Star Line commissioned, refitted and renamed her GREYHOUND. The dining room crew consisted of a steward and a combination of 60 cooks and waiters. She continued in service until the new GREYHOUND was commissioned in 1902. The new GREYHOUND, 276 feet overall with a 68-foot beam, was built of steel at Wyandotte and launched on February 16, 1902. From Wyandotte, she was towed by the steamer PROMISE and the tug C.A. LORMAR to Detroit where her cabins were finished and she received her machinery.

ARROW - built of wood at Trenton in 1848. The reproduction above is from a photograph (Courtesy Burton Collection) of a painting by Robert Hopkin dated 1855. In the 1850's, the ARROW competed intensely with the FORESTER and PEARL for the Detroit-Port Huron passenger business. An 1860 news clipping on file at the Burton Historical Collection promoted a 25 cent fare which included the entertainment of a band. In 1863 the ARROW was sold to parties on Lake Superior, but later that year she was condemned at Green Bay, Wisconsin. Another ARROW was built In 1889 and ran between Sandusky and the Lake Erie Islands until 1922.

PEARL - (Courtesy Burton Collection) 160-foot built at Ward's* Shipyard of Marine City in 1851, specifically for the Detroit-Port Huron route. Retired in 1867, she was dismantled in 1869. PEARL was powered by a 34-inch cylinder, 9-foot stroke, beam engine.

*In 1818, Captain Samuel Ward and Father Gabriel Richard founded what was to become Marine City. By the time of his death in 1854, Samuel Ward had amassed a fortune of nearly one million (1854) dollars invested in railroad and bank stocks, real estate holdings and particularly ships and shipyards. In his last eight years, he and his nephew Eber Ward reportedly built twenty-two steamers, including the FORESTER, PEARL and the SAMUEL WARD. Eber Brock Ward became Michigan's first steel magnate and produced the first ingots of "Bessemer" steel in the U.S. at his Wyandotte plant.

31

IDLEWILD - the 232-foot iron hull was built at Wyandotte in 1879 and extended to 284 feet at Cleveland in 1889. Originally named the GRACE McMILLAN, after the daughter of W.C. McMillan, she was renamed as IDLEWILD in 1881. In 1903 she was decommissioned by the White Star Line and was returned to the estate of Darius Cole. From 1905 she ran the Buffalo-Crystal Beach route along with the steamer DARIUS COLE. In 1914 she was dismantled at Detroit.

UNIQUE – the 175-foot wooden hull and cabins were built by Alexander Anderson at Marine City in 1894. Four watertight cross bulkheads divided the bright yellow hull into five compartments.

The UNIQUE was designed, owned and operated by Crocket McElroy. Mr. McElroy aimed to build a boat that would have a maximum speed of 24 mile an hour and a reliable cruising speed of 20 miles an hour. He also wanted it to be strong, sturdy and capable of carrying 500 passengers comfortably. Every effort was put forward to make this a first class ship.

This was the fastest excursion boat on the lakes, as her owner and builder had intended, but she was never dependable and was often passed up by the slower steamers as she drifted aimlessly waiting for the boilers to be repaired. On May 13, 1895, one of her boilers exploded killing the engineer, stoker and firemen. Forty passengers were aboard and all escaped injury.

In 1896 the UNIQUE was reported sold to Cuban revolutionaries as a blockade runner, but the deal was canceled. In 1901 she was operating on Lake Ontario before being sold again to run on the river from Philadelphia and renamed the DIAMOND STATE. In 1903 she became the private yacht of August Belmonte of New York City and renamed SATELLITE. In 1915, she burned in New York Harbor and the hull was later used as a barge.

Note: Crocket McElroy was one of the St. Clair River District's most illustrious and energetic pioneers. McElroy at one time was a stove and salt manufacturer, timber ranger, mayor the city of St. Clair, state senator and shipbuilder. Another popular excursion steamer built and operated by McElroy was the MARY, which was also noted for her exceptional speed.

OWANA - The 200-foot steel hull was built at Wyandotte in 1891 and was originally named PENNSYLVANIA. In 1904, she was commissioned by the White Star Line and was renamed OWANA, after the sweetheart of the Indian Chief "Tashmoo." She had been renamed ERIE by 1929 when the Ecorse boat yard of Captain Wm. Nicholson exploded in flames. The OWANA, FRANK E. KIRBY, SAPPHO and a tug were destroyed. (Courtesy Dossin Great Lakes Museum)

MILTON D. WARD - built in 1870 at the Ward's Shipyard of Marine City. The Free Press on May 4, 1875, reported that the Star Line Flagship had made her first trip of that season. In 1892 the tired wooden ship was leased to the Health Board for two years to be used as a smallpox hospital and quarantine station. She was laid up near the intake of the Detroit water system and was never used again. Fire finished her off in 1894. Later the lines were cut and the charred hull sank a short distance away.

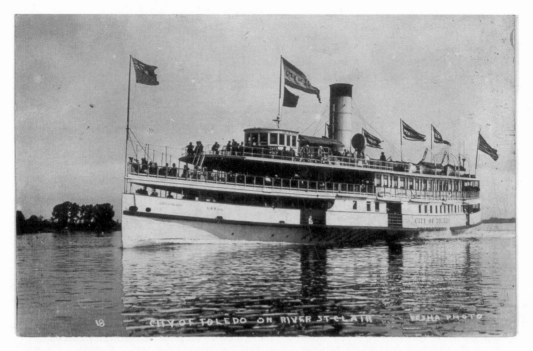

CITY OF TOLEDO – the 212-foot steel hull was built in 1891 at Toledo and extended to 252 feet at Detroit in 1916. She was destroyed by fire at New York in 1932.

The FRANK E. KIRBY was named for the era's most prominent and prolific naval architect. Built in 1890, she was destroyed by fire in 1929 along with the OWANA.

NORTH AMERICAN.   PESHA PHOTO

Detroiters were also able to enjoy many of the finest "Overnight" passenger ships ever built. Among the many were the NORTH AMERICAN, CITY OF ERIE, EASTERN STATES and the S. S. HAMONIC. The NORTH AMERICAN cruised the middle lakes from 1913 to 1963. The slightly larger twin, SOUTH AMERICAN, continued until 1967. The D&C Line operated from the 1850s to the 1950s.

BLT/898 CITY OF ERIE   PESHA PHOTO Scrap 1941

EASTERN STATES   8   PESHA PHOTO

Northern Navigation Co.
LIMITED

New S. S. Hamonic
Finest, Largest and Fastest Passenger and Freight Steamship on the Great Lakes

Tours of the Great Lakes and Georgian Bay
Three Trips Weekly from Sarnia

Mondays, Wednesdays and Saturdays

At 4:15 P. M. Eastern Standard Time
Making Direct Connections with White Star Steamers from Detroit

SAMPLE FARES

Detroit to Sault Ste. Marie and Return	-	-	-	-	-	$18.40
" " Port Arthur " "	-	-	-	-	-	34.40
" " Duluth " "	-	-	-	-	-	39.40
" " Collingwood " "	-	-	-	-	-	36.60

Meals and Berths Included on Northern Navigation Co. Steamers

Other Trips Through the 30,000 Islands, Beautiful Georgian Bay and Lake Superior

A Veritable Fresh Water Sea Voyage of 1,500 Miles

Tickets on Sale by all White Star Line Agents
For Literature and Information Apply to any Agency or

E. W. HOLTON
Eastern Passenger Agent, SARNIA, ONT.

C. F. BIELMAN, Traffic Mgr.
White Star Line, DETROIT, MICH.

37

April 1, 1895
(Newspaper unknown)

FLATS!

Promise Tried to Go There Yesterday,

But She Got No Frather Than the Old Club Dock.

Ice In the Lake Was 18 Inches Thick,

But Through It the Steamer Plowed Steadily.

Passengers Walked On the Ice Ahead.

A Few Daring Ones Reached the Rushmere.

The steamer Promise took about 150 pasesngers fairly within sight of their promised land, the St. Clair Flats, yesterday, but allowed only a few to enjoy the pleasures of the particular spot they desired to set foot upon. To do even this occupied over four hours' time, for on the up trip the boat for fifteen miles plowed through ice from eight to eighteen inches thick. Once only was the Promise stuck, but eventually she made a landing at the Old Club dock, going no further. The boat was not in good condition to battle with the ice, two blades of her wheel having been broken.

It was a quarter to 10 when the gang plank of the boat was raised, and the first trip to the Flats for 1895 attempted. All was plain sailing until the head of Belle Isle was reached, where across the channel, from the light house to Peche Island a great mass of ice stretched, anchored firmly to both shores, and on the lower side of which duck hunters had erected "blinds" of chunks of ice, and spread their decoys temptingly along its edge. But the, Promise thrust her nose into the mass and quickly made a channel for herself into the open water beyond.

At the dummy light another streak of ice was met, probably a mile in width, and from four to six inches thick. Along the lower edge of this cake a solitary duck hunter had fixed his ice "blind" and was waiting patiently in the cold for a few shots at the ducks which rose and flew toward the Canadian shore where could be caught occasional glimpses of clear water. At a six mile gait the boat made her way through this obstruction, when a liberal patch of clear water was reached. But beyond this, for fifteen miles, the Promise had to battle with ice from a foot to a foot and a half thick. Occasionally she stopped, as if to rest. Then the passengers would clamber down her sides and take a slide on the ice. At one time over thirty took a stroll, some even staying until the boat started, and then on a dog trot keeping up with her. The path she cut was so clean that the ice on either side did not seem in the least disturbed. One of the men, in a spirit of bravado, actually trotted in front of the boat, at one time placing his hand on the bow as he walked along. A measurement with a rule showed the ice to be seventeen inches thick, but the under side was considerably honeycombed.

Took Many Snap Shots.

There were a score of hand cameras aboard, and half a dozen of the more venturesome took snap shots of the boat from the ice, a couple even staying out until she had begun to move, in order to get a picture of the boat in motion. Luckily there was no air holes thereabouts, or the attempt might not have had so pleasant an ending.

When within two miles of the piers, open water was again reached, which continued to the head of the canal, where an almost impenetrable jam prevented further progress with any hopes of getting through before night. So after tying to the Old Club dock, Captain Campbell announced that the boat would go no further. It was then a quarter after 2 and four and a half hours had been consumed in making the twenty-six miles.

A few daring spirits, urged to the attempt by their desire to see their Flats property after the long winter, attempted the task of getting further up stream by walking along the shore and trusting to luck to get them

the side cuts and creeks that afford in summer, easy passage from the river into the bay. The Tribune man went along to see the fun, and was amply repaid. Boards and ladders were seized and stretched across the rotting ice, and over these improvised bridges the crowd slid and stumbled and got an occasional wetting. It took the boat the best part of an hour to reach the Rushmere, where the last one, giving a "long lingering look" in the direction of the Peninsular Club, the Riverside and Joe Bedore's, reluctantly turned back. Will Warren stuck his plans for an enlarged and beautified Riverside Hotel into his pocket and made some remarks not in the revised version. These were seconded and passed viva voce, and all were soon on their way back. But in the meantime before all had crossed the last ditch, one of the improvised bridges floated away, necessitating a call on a friendly hunter, who dragged his duck boat across the marsh to their rescue, enabling them to reach the Promise just in time to make the return trip.

The Trip Back.

While it took two hours and a half to reach the Flats, it only took a little over two hours to come back; for the old path remained open until nearly past Windmill lighthouse. There the ice had shifted, sweeping away the duck shooters' "blinds," and carrying the open water to the south.

It was half past 6 o'clock when the final straggler stepped ashore at the foot of Woodward avenue. This was an hour ahead of schedule time; but the general observation was made that it was better to be home by daylight than drifting around Lake St. Clair in a disabled boat on a mighty cold night, even if it was the last day in March.

Among those on board the Promise were William and J. Frank Boydell, Andrew Smith, Charles Sullivan, Joseph Sparks, Fred E. Butler, John M. Eberts, E. C. Whitney, E. G. Myrick, George Gibson, John Gies, Joseph L. Koester, John Grogan, W. H. Warren, Senator Smalley, Charles Coulter, Alfred E. Brush, George H. Lothrop, Frank G. Curtis, Henry P. McDonnell, Alfred Easter, T. J. Riley, William J. Burton, John J. Marten, O. K. Mulford, Tom Bradbier, Frank B. Wherrey, John Walker, James Roach, Joseph Deiderich, S. S. Babcock, George Johnson, John Higgins, Henry Woodlock, Charles Gagnier, Albert Strelow and William Linderman.

DETROIT, BELLE ISLE & WINDSOR FERRY COMPANY

The competing Detroit – Windsor ferry companies consolidated in 1877 as the Detroit and Windsor Ferry Association combing the steamers HOPE (built in 1870), VICTORIA (1872), FORTUNE (1875) and EXCELSIOR (1876) under one administration. Later additions included GARLAND (1880), SAPPHO (1883, formerly of the Walkerville and Detroit Ferry Company), PROMISE (1892), PLEASURE (1894), BRITANNIA (1906), LA SALLE (1922), CADILLAC (1928) and two created for and dedicated to the "Bob-Lo" run, COLUMBIA (1901), and STE. CLAIR (1911), both designed by Frank E. Kirby.

In 1878 the Detroit Dry Dock Co. purchased the assets of the association and in 1883 sold them to a group headed by Capt. John Pridgeon. When the City of Detroit turned Belle Isle into a playground the Ferry Company added the new route and changed its name to Detroit, Belle Isle & Windsor Ferry Company (DBI&WFC)*. In 1891 Walter E. Campbel (one of the original members of the 1877 association) and his associates gained control of the company. It remained in the hands of Campbell and his managerial successors until 1939.

DBI&WFC was usually the first to send its ships across Lake St. Clair in the spring, as early as mid-March.** On March 31, 1895 the PROMISE made the first run with 150 passengers eager to inspect their properties on the St. Clair Flats. The related newspaper clipping is reprinted on the preceding page.

From the beginning DBI&WFC offered excursions in addition to regularly scheduled crossings between Detroit, Belle Isle and

*Around 1912 "Belle Isle' was removed from the company name, the route's importance having been replaced by street cars' easy access. After the last ferry left from Woodward Avenue on July 18, 1938, the name changed again, becoming the bob-Lo Excursion Company
**The White Star Lines paddle-wheeled fleet could not operate safely until all the ice was cleared from the water.

Windsor. Between 1877 and 1887 one of the more popular trips from Detroit was the boat ride to the mineral springs a few miles below Windsor. (However, when the flow of "curative" sulfur waters stopped, the site was forgotten.) During the same period, the company ferried excursionists to an amusement park called Brighton Beach just below the mineral springs. Between 1892 and 1895, the company ran excursions to Hotel Des-Chree-Shos-Ka on Fighting Island. Both the DBI&WFC and the Walkerville and Detroit Ferry Company regularly scheduled moonlight rides into Lake St. Clair and day journeys to the mouth of the St. Clair river.

In 1897 DBI&WFC purchased 10 acres on Bois Blanc (Bob-Lo) Island and made improvements. On June 20, 1898, ferry service began to Bois Blanc Park. Over the next 3 years the company purchased an additional 10 acres and the name was subsequently changed to Bob-Lo to deal with the English speaking public's inability to pronounce the original French name.

From 1905 – 1910 the company leased Russell Island, on the St. Clair River, and operated Camp Algonac. In 1911 the company purchased Peche Island with the intention of developing a park for " the more desirable element of pleasure seekers.*" The park was never developed, but Mr. Campbell made his summer home on the island and died there in 1923. By then there was ho interest in additional amusement parks.

After the Detroit-Windsor Tunnel and then the Ambassador Bridge were built, demand for ferry service was greatly reduced. In 1938 the Detroit & Windsor Ferry Company had completed its government contract and requested permission to discontinue service. Service ended July 19. The next year the Chicago, Duluth, Georgian Bay Transit Company purchased the park and the two remaining steamers. Strategically, it was intended that the new company's steamers, NORTH and SOUTH AMERICAN, would be able to land at the Woodward Bob-Lo dock.

In 1949 Troy H. Browning purchased the Bob-Lo business and operated the Bob-Lo Company until 1979 when a seven-member group bought the company. After only two years the company filed for bankruptcy protection and in 1983 AAA of Michigan bought the assets.

AAA made substantial improvements before selling the business again in 1988. Unfortunately, after a number of "mishaps" the new company filed for bankruptcy protection and the steamers COLUMBIA and ST. CLAIR were retired at the close of the regular season in 1991. The park closed for good at the end of the regular season in 1993. The park has been dismantled and the land subdivided for new homes. The boats sit idle, however, there is still optimism that one of them may someday be restored.

*Evening Record, Windsor, August 26, 1913.

The following caricatures,

"OUR FRIENDS
AS WE SEE 'EM"

Originally appeared in

A Gallery of Pen Sketches
In Black and White of
Our Michigan Friends
"As We See 'Em"

by the
Newspaper Cartoonists' Association of Michigan
1905

TRUMAN H. NEWBERRY
SECRETARY OF THE NAVY
LIEUTENANT ON U.S.S. YOSEMITE
MEMBER INSTITUTE OF
NAVAL ARCHITECTS.
NUMEROUS BUSINESS INTERESTS.

FRANK E. KIRBY
CONSULTING ENGINEER
DESIGNER OF NUMEROUS STEAMERS INCLUDING
THE TASHMOO, CITY OF DETROIT III AND COLUMBIA

CHARLES F. BIELMAN
SECRETARY AND TRAFFIC MANAGER WHITE STAR LINE
SECRETARY AND TREASURER THE STEWART TRANSPORTATION CO.
PRESIDENT BOARD OF COMMERCE

AARON A. PARKER
PRESIDENT WHITE STAR LINE
TREASURER PARKER BROS. LTD.
TREASURER AND MANAGER BUFFALO DETROIT TRANSPORTATION CO.
DIRECTOR DIME SAVINGS BANK

BYRON W. PARKER
GENERAL MANAGER WHITE STAR LINE
PRESIDENT PARKER BROS. CO., LTD.
PRESIDENT MONARCH COAL AND MINERAL CO.

EDWARD A. DUSTIN
ASHLEY & DUSTIN, STEAMER AGENTS
PROPRIETORS OF STR. FRANK E. KIRBY
AGENTS WYANDOTTE AND ALGOMAH CENTRAL STEAMSHIP LINE

WILLIAM LIVINGSTONE
PRESIDENT LAKE CARRIERS' ASSOCIATION
PRESIDENT DIME SAVINGS BANK
PUBLISHER DETROIT JOURNAL

MICHAEL J. MURPHY
PRESIDENT MURPHY CHAIR CO.
PRESIDENT SECURITY TRUST CO.,
DIRECTOR PEOPLES STATE BANK AND
MICHIGAN SAVINGS BANK
FIRST PRESIDENT DETROIT BOARD OF COMMERCE

ORA J. MULFORD
PRESIDENT GRAY MOTOR CO.
PRESIDENT O. J. MULFORD ADV. CO.
PRESIDENT MICHIGAN STREET CAR ADV. CO.

GEORGE HENDRIE
SECRETARY AND TREASURER GROSSE POINTE LANDS CO.
SERVED ABOARD U.S.S. YOSEMITE
WITH FAMILY HAS BEEN CLOSELY ASSOCIATED WITH ALL FORMS OF COMMERCIAL TRANSPORTATION,
INCLUDING DETROIT & BUFFALO STEAMBOAT CO.

JOHN PRIDGEON, JR.
OFFICER & DIRECTOR WHITE STAR LINE
DIRECTOR DETROIT & MILWAUKEE R.R. AND THE DIME SAVING BANK
MAYOR OF DETROIT 1889-90
(WITH HIS FATHER, CAPT. JOHN PRIDGEON, FORMERLY OPERATED THE
CHICAGO & SARNIA LINE AND OWNED THE DETROIT, BELLE ISLE & WINDSOR
FERRY BOAT COMPANY, 1883-1891)

FREDERICK D. STANDISH
SERVED ON U.S.S. YOSEMITE
TREASURER KURTZ PAPER BOX COMPANY
COMMANDER OF THE NAVAL MILITIA OF MICHIGAN.

HENRY B. JOY
SERVED ON U.S.S. YOSEMITE
PRESIDENT PACKARD MOTOR CAR CO.

FRANKLIN H. WALKER
Hiram Walker & Sons, Ltd.
Walkerville and Detroit Ferry Company

JOHN STEVENSON
STEAMBOAT AGENT

CHAS. W. THOMPSON
ST. CLAIR
SALT
MANAGER, THOMPSON LINE

U. S. S. YOSEMITE

In addition to recreational and commercial shipping, another of Detroit's nautical branches was represented by the Michigan Naval Brigade founded in 1897. Its Commander, Detroit Industrialist Truman H. Newberry, was one of two Michigan crew members of the U. S. S. YOSEMITE (Yosemite) who went on to become the Secretary of the Navy. The other was Edwin Denby.

When Spain was forced to declare war on the U. S., April 24, the U. S. hastily assembled and converted 126 merchant ships into the U. S. Auxiliary Naval Forces. One of the ships was the 389-foot cargo ship from New Orleans, converted from freighter to fighter and renamed the U. S. S. YOSEMITE (the first of three navy vessels to be so named). Except for four regular navy officers, 14 officers and the 267 enlisted men were volunteers from Michigan. Many of the men were students, alumni and faculty of the University of Michigan and many came from the ranks of Detroit's social elite. (Of note, the Secretary of War at the time was Detroiter Russell A. Alger.)

The YOSEMITE's first mission was to serve as escort for landing Marines on Guantanamo, where the first land battle was fought. Her last mission of the war, was to be the blockade of San Juan, Puerto Rico. While attacking and disabling a cargo ship trying to enter the harbor, the Yosemite entered the range of the harbor canons and was being pursued by three small Spanish war ships. The Spanish shells were bracketing the Yosemite as she tacked furiously to break free. A sudden and intense tropical rainstorm obscured her from the Spanish canons and allowed her to escape with only a soaked crew and some self-inflicted damage, mostly from munitions exploding prematurely, and one of the 20 fires experienced during the entire cruise.

No other ship in the U. S. Navy had so many well-educated and prominent sailors. It may be interesting to speculate on what might have happened to Detroit industry, in particular the automobile industry, if some of the Spanish shells had hit their target. Among others, the crew of the Yosemite included the following:

Truman H. Newberry	-Extensive business interests, Secretary of the Navy and U. S. Senator.
Henry B. Joy	-President Packard Motor Company
J. Walter Drake	-President Hupp Motor Car Company.
Charles B. King	-President King Motor Car Company, builder of the first automobile in Detroit and the first commercially successful 4-cycle engine in the country, plus numerous other innovations.
William A. Livingstone	-General manager and founder of the Detroit Publishing Company.
Albert Henry Stanley	-Executive with Detroit United Railway. Later reorganized the London subway system and was knighted Sir Albert by King George V.
Charles F. Hammond	-President Hammond, Standish & Co., meat packing, and President Hammond Building Company (built the city's first skyscraper)
George Hendrie	-Sec/Treas Grosse Pointe Lands Co. (Brother was an ensign in U. S. Navy)
Frederick D. Standish	-Treasurer Kurtz Paper Box Co. (Brother to James of Hammond & Standish)
Edwin Denby	-U. S. Congressman, Secretary of the Navy (namesake of Detroit's Denby H. S.)
Mortimer Cooley	-Dean of U of M Faculty of the School of Engineering & Architecture (24 years)
Willis E. Buhl	-President Buhl Sons Co. and Buhl Stamping Co.
D. B. Duffield	-Lawyer

POST CARDS IN AMERICA

A brief history

Introduction

Deltiology, from the Greek word meaning small stone writing tablet, is the formal name for post card collecting. The popularity and broad subject range have made post card collecting one of the most important collectible hobbies in the world.

The Civil War of 1861-1865 had given photography a powerful impetus. Mathew Brady and his photographs had proven that outdoor pictures were not only possible but that the public had a strong interest in them. Advertisers began issuing millions of picture cards, and sets of Souvenir Views went on sale in the leading cities, resorts, and other places where sightseers congregated. Several firms were formed to supply and publish these photos.

Due to government postal regulations, post cards were a long time in developing. While few U.S. collections begin earlier than the souvenir cards sold at the 1893 World's Columbian Exposition in Chicago, the origin may be envelopes with pictures printed on them dating to the mid-1800's. Privately printed "postal cards," requiring regular first class postage, began appearing about the same time.

1873 – Present: Postal Cards

The major difference between a "post card" and a "postal card" is that, while both are sent through the U.S. Post Office, a post card must have a stamp or other postage added. A postal card is purchased in the Post Office and already has postage printed on it. Postal cards have been printed by the US government since 1873.

1893 – 1898: Souvenir Cards

While there were some earlier issues, most collections begin no earlier than the cards sold at the Columbian Exposition in Chicago in 1893. These included both illustrations on government-printed postal cards and privately printed "souvenir" cards. The postal cards had the government's 1-cent stamp pre-printed while the privately printed cards required a 2-cent stamp to be applied separately. Writing was not permitted on the address side of either card.

1898 – 1901: Private Mailing Cards

Although the 1893 World's Columbian Exposition in Chicago and a few similar public shows had published Souvenir Mailing Cards, the public had not popularly accepted their use and the earliest individual attempts at publication had not been successful. European publishers of the late 1800's had met a somewhat better reception and some of their attractive cards reaching this country had a stimulating effect. Congress took note of the trend and on May 19, 1898 an Act of Congress granted private printers permission to print and sell cards that bore the inscription "Private Mailing Card." The Private Mailing Card could now be mailed for 1 cent, with an adhesive stamp. It was soon apparent that the Private Mailing Card would become a popular addition to American life. However, still, no writing was allowed on the address side.

A small space was available on the front at the bottom of the image for a message, as writing on the back was not yet authorized. The back of the cards carried the required inscription, "Private Mailing Card Authorized by Act of Congress of May 19, 1898."

1901 – 1907: Post Cards

On December 24, 1901 the government granted the right to private printers to use the words "POST CARD." This is the era of the "undivided back," as writing was still not permitted on the address side. During this period individuals began to have their own black & white photographs printed on paper with postcard backs.

Small space was still provided on the front for messages. Only the address and the inscription "Post Card" were allowed on the undivided back.

During this period England, France and Germany began permitting "divided backs" in 1902, 1904 and 1905, respectively.

1907 – 1914: Divided Back Era

On March 1, 1907 the U. S. Government permitted postcards with divided backs. With this innovation, the left side of the back could be used for writing messages and images could fill the front of the card. As in the past, most color post cards during this period were printed in Europe or under license with the Swiss and German patent holders.

The almost universal acceptance of divided-back post cards ushered in the "Golden Era" of post cards with millions being sold, used and collected. This was the era of peak popularity for souvenir post cards and the most important American color post card printer through this period was the Detroit Publishing Company (DPC), see separate chapter. In 1897 an affiliate of DPC obtained the exclusive U.S. rights to the Photochrom process from the Swiss owners. They produced high quality color post cards with views of local, national and international interest.

1915 – 1930: The White Border Era
With the advent of World War I the supply of German color post cards came to an end. Increasing cost of production, inexperience and changing public tastes led to the production of poor quality cards. To save ink, a border was left around the image. High competition in a shrinking market caused many publishers to go out of business. In this era it became common to include longer descriptions and add them on the back of the cards. In 1925 the postage rate for post cards was increased to 2 cents while postal cards remained at 1 cent. In 1928 the postcard rate was reset to match the postal card rate of 1 cent.

Except for the white border, the front on many cards from this era look similar to early divided backs. However, a deterioration of the color quality was becoming the norm. Except for the addition of longer descriptions, the backs of these cards also look very similar to the previous divided back era.

1930 – 1944: Linen Era
New printing processes allowed printing on cards with a high rag content that resulted in a noticeable linen-like finish.

1939 – Present: Modern Photochrome
"Chrome" cards were first introduced in 1939 by Union Oil Company for sale in their western service stations. By 1944 they were widespread and have been the most popular type of post card up to the present.

The last 1-cent postal card and post card were mailed by December 31, 1951. They became 20 cents on January 1, 1995, and are now 24 cents.

Below, Crockett McElroy's STR. CLARA — built in 1860 and rebuilt in 1887. For many years she ferried passengers between St. Clair and Courtright, Ontario.

REAL PHOTO CARDS

An Introduction

Real Photo Cards (RPC) began to appear almost as soon as private post cards were authorized. Many are one of a kind while others were produced in modest mass quantities, usually by the photographer in a studio.

A caption was often hand etched on the negative. Some of them included the name of the photographer and a reference number. Then the image was printed on a post card back. Generally the captions on the one-of-a-kind cards are not as neat as the "mass" produced cards. (Writing in reverse took some practice.)

LOUIS PESHA
And The Pesha Post Card Company

For collectors of early images from the areas around the Detroit and St. Clair Rivers, the most important RPC printer was the Pesha Post Card Co. However, very little is known about the man behind the company, Louis Pesha.

Pesha operated in the Oil Spring area of Ontario from 1899 to about 1902 when he moved to Marine City, Michigan. There are no known undivided back post cards by Pesha, so he may have been a portrait photographer prior to 1907. All of his known post cards were produced from 1907 to his death in September 1912. Many of his works continued to be printed by his wife until 1920. Those are real post cards, but they have a white border and are of a poorer quality than the pre-1913 cards produced under Mr. Pesha's supervision.

In addition to the description, number and his name etched in the negative, some of the backs carried the name and address of his company. In addition to the Marine City address, a Detroit address began appearing in 1910.

Note, a group of Pesha collectors in Michigan has undertaken the task of establishing a database of his cards. To assist this project you are encouraged to send a list of existing cards including description, number and location, if available, to:
Donald R. Wilson, c/o Flushing Area Historical Society, P.O. Box 87, Flushing, MI 48433 or Email: drmewilson@worldnet.att.net

63

THE DETROIT PUBLISHING COMPANY[1]

A Brief History

In the early 1890's Photochrom, a new photolithographic process, had been developed in Switzerland for reproducing pictures in color. In 1896 a group of Detroit businessmen were organizing a company to publish photographs and sent Edwin H. Husher to Switzerland to study the process.

Mr. Husher was an established photographer and well known for his California scenes. The managing member of the business group was William Allan Livingstone, a vessel agent and marine engineer. His father, William Livingstone, was a well known banker and publisher and was closely associated with the shipping interests in the Great Lakes since the beginning of his active career[2].

At the recommendation of Mr. Husher, in the summer of 1896, W. A Livingstone began corresponding with the famous landscape photographer William Henry Jackson with the idea of absorbing the W. H. Jackson Company. Mr. Jackson had several important things to contribute: the most complete set of Western negatives yet assembled[3], his experience and his reputation. Born in 1843, Jackson's artistic talents landed him a job doing retouching work in a photographic studio in 1858 and he had been in the business ever since. (Mr. Jackson's autobiography, *Time Exposure*, is a history of early photography and the exciting life of a man who was active until a short time before he died in New York, in 1942, at the age of 99.)

During the summer of 1897 Mr. Livingstone went to Zurich to complete negotiations and conclude a contract for the North American rights with Photoglob, the Swiss owner of the Photochrom process. In Detroit, the Photochrom Company (PC) had already been organized[4] to exploit the process and a new factory to produce color prints was nearing completion. In the fall of 1897 Mr. Livingstone went to Denver and negotiated the merger of the W.H. Jackson Company. This included the acquisition of some 10,000 glass plate negatives. Mr. Jackson received stock in PC, became a director and a valued employee.

The organization also needed a trained staff. Mr. Albert V. Schuler, an expert printer from Switzerland, was persuaded to assemble a team and move to Detroit. Mr. and Mrs. Schuler, an artist, machinist and two operators proceeded to Detroit and set up the process.

The new enterprise supplied photographs for all purposes especially for use in books, magazines, and advertising specialties such as calendars and blotters. Many of the prints were of large framing size or suitable for long advertising hangers in the custom of the day. The firm made a specialty of religious prints and did much work with churches and religious orders. Their line of glass lantern slides was one of the best in the country and extensively used for lectures and educational purposes. So, when the Souvenir Views were combined with Postal Cards to become Souvenir Mailing Cards, it was only natural that the company would include this in their line of business.

For a few years after Jackson joined the company he continued his photographic work, traveling throughout the country. In 1902 he toured the Southwest in a special railroad car, known as the "California Special", containing a photographic studio and gallery. The car was sponsored by the Santa Fe Railroad and PC's affiliate, the Detroit Photographic Company, another Livingstone enterprise. The gallery displayed prints, cards, and other PC products.

In 1903 Husher sold his interest in the company and bought a California orange grove. As a result, Jackson became plant manager in charge of production and at the age of 60 retired from the rigors of field work.

After 1905 the PC name was dropped and the public Detroit Publishing Company (DPC) name was used exclusively. At the time the business was at the pinnacle of its prosperity, employing about 40 artisans and a dozen traveling photographers. It turned out about 7 million prints annually in all sizes from post cards to large framing pictures. In addition to its Detroit properties, it opened sales rooms in New York, Boston and Los Angeles, had representatives in many other cities and exchange agreements with the Swiss company and the English licensee.

Post cards became a big part of their business as the public finally recognized them as ideal souvenirs and greetings. In addition, clubs were organized everywhere by post card collectors and the demand skyrocketed. For the next few years post card collecting was almost a universal hobby and so many were saved that even today many cards of the period are more common than the later ones. With their superb stock of negatives, the Detroit Company was in an unequaled position to take advantage of this demand.

During the second decade of the century other publishers, using less expensive printing methods, made it difficult to compete for the post card trade but an acknowledged superior product enabled the company to hold on to a sustaining core of business. While the post card business gradually declined in volume other lines of work made it possible to keep the firm in a prosperous condition.

Business slowed considerably during World War I. The federal government categorized their process as non-essential to the war effort, making it difficult to acquire material or keep workers employed. In the flash of almost universal prosperity that followed World War I the company again prospered. However, the recession of 1920-21 dealt the crippling blow from which the firm never fully recovered. When William A. Livingstone died in 1924 it was necessary to retrench and wind up most of its business. For the next eight years, under receivership, William's brother Robert[5] attempted to carry on and the company continued to do limited business. This was almost entirely devoted to the selling of the more than 2,000,000 postcards and prints remaining on hand.

The Great Depression made further efforts useless and a final liquidation of the firm's assets began in 1932. Robert died in 1936 and in 1937 the remaining material, including some 40,000 glass negatives, were rescued by Edsel Ford for the Edison Institute, now known as Henry Ford Museum & Greenfield Village. Subsequently, owing to the efforts of William Jackson's son Clarence, the institute donated the negatives of Western views to the Colorado Historical Society. The negatives for sites east of the Mississippi were donated to the U. S. Library of Congress in Washington, D.C. The institute's remaining collection includes over 30,000 vintage photographic prints, 5,000 color and sepia lithograph prints and some 15,000 postcards.

The great Detroit Publishing Company may have become a thing of the past, but it will be remembered forever through these collections and the millions of post cards preserved by collectors.

The Printing Process

The Detroit Publishing Company's (DPC) Photochrom was a Swiss invention and the process was carefully guarded, the DPC being the only printer in this country authorized to use it in North America. The exact method was never revealed and even today, experts in the graphic arts do not know the full details. It is known as a "asphaltum" process, the picture being printed from finely grained lithographic stones with an asphalt coating. Continuous tone negatives are used exclusively, with no half-tone screen. One reason for the many varieties is that the plate had a very limited life after being placed on the press. However, they could be polished off and regrained. A minimum of four stones was used for each print and occasionally as many as fourteen, which gave the prints the fine color values. The stones came from Bavaria. The process was complicated, lengthy, and painstaking, requiring three or four times the usual amount of man-hours to prepare a single card for the pressman. That is the reason the firm could not meet cheaper competition in a falling market.

The word "Phostint" like "Photochrom" is a trade word descriptive of a printing method. Phostint is usually used in reference to the later issues of the company after about 1907. However, there is evidence that it was used from the very beginning although it does not appear on the early cards. An advertising brochure by the company copyrighted in 1914 states "Phostint is the grade of quality in view post cards. They have been circulated throughout the United States during the past fifteen years".

This effectively dates the first Phostint as 1899 and indicates that the word was used from that time. A 1903 catalogue states in bold type that the cards are "Published in Phostint" and "by our exclusive Phostint process". Before 1899 the word "Photochrom" appears to have been used exclusively for color photolithographic prints.

Phostint was probably a slight variation from the original Photochrom method. It does not closely resemble the issues of either the London or Swiss firms. It was not a permanent process but was improved from time to time. Collectors can easily discern three distinct phases by merely looking at the cards. The dates are difficult to give exactly, due to reprinting, but the early cards to about 1905 show softly graduated color tones. Then to about 1908 comes much sharper and stronger coloring. After that comes, what may be called a blending of the two, which may be acclaimed as the supreme achievement in post card coloring. These are the cards best known as Phostint because by that time the word was featured in fairly large type on the backs of the cards. Among them are many reprintings of the earlier cards.

1. At various times different affiliated names were associated with the business: The Photochrom Company, Detroit Photographic Company and the Detroit Publishing Company (DPC). The first annual report of The Photochrom Co. was filed with the State of Michigan in 1898, for 1897, and they continued to be filed through 1922. However, after 1905 that name was dropped from promotional and product identification. The name most frequently used is DPC. DPC may have been an assumed name of The Photochrom Co., or another affiliate, as no annual reports appear to be filed under that name.

Another affiliated entity, Detroit Photographic Co., filed annual reports through 1909 stating that its purpose was to sell prints and art goods from its retail store address in Detroit. After 1909 they continued to be filed for the purpose of protecting the name.

While the use of the affiliated names is not completely clear, it is certain that the distinctive process of The Photochrom Co. came from a license technique from the Photoglob Company of Zurich, Switzerland, who was also a shareholder. Today, the affiliated enterprise is popularly referred to simply as the Detroit Publishing Company.

2. The senior Livingstone, William (no middle name) Livingstone, Jr., was born in Dundas, Ontario, 1844 and died in Detroit, 1925. For over 23 years he was the President of the Lakes Carriers Association. The Livingstone Channel[a] in the Detroit River and the Lighthouse[b] at Belle Isle are named in his honor.

> *a. The Livingstone channel increased the Detroit River's minimum depth from 12 to 22 feet. Since the late 1870s, the treacherous section of the river known as "Lime Kiln Crossing" was continuously excavated, but the river's swift current eradicated any progress. It was not until new technologies couldbe applied that the long-standing problem could by eliminated. After 4 years of dredging, the challel was completed in 1912.*

> *b. The William Livingstone Memorial Light was completed in 1929 on the east end of Belle Isle to honor the navigational achievements made under the leadership of Mr. Livingstone, a former Belle Isle Commissioner. The lighthouse designed by Albert Kahn with a distinctive Art Deco style is the only marble lighthouse in the world and one of only two in the U.S. built as a memorial.*

3. Jackson's collection of some 10,000 negatives was added to

Husher's California collection and Livingstone's file of Great Lakes shipping photographs. The enterprise was able to begin with an extensive and wide-ranging photographic archive.

4. Organizing began by the time Husher went to Switzerland in 1896, incorporation occurred in 1897.

5. Robert Bruce Livingstone, younger brother of William A., was associated with the business since inception. Robert is remembered as an excellent salesman. Among his most important clients were the Metropolitan Museum in New York, the Philadelphia Museum of Art and other museums, which gave the company the sole right to make color reproductions of their paintings. Another was Fred Harvey, owner of a chain of restaurants along the route of the Santa Fe Railroad, who ordered large quantities of post cards with Southwestern scenic attractions. Rovbert's wife Grace wrote many of the captions for the cards, as well as short descriptive leaflets to accompany cards sold in sets.

Note: DPC also published Real Photo Cards. In every example known to the author the views available as Real Photo Cards were also available as color post cards. Only the color versions were selected for this publication.

– COLOR TOUR –
TOLEDO to PORT HURON

A SUMMER CRUISE ABOARD
THE WHITE STAR LINE SQUADRON

Sit back, enjoy the breeze and watch the scenes unfold as we ride the waves from Toledo to Port Huron. Then, when you are ready for the detail, come back for a narrated tour. Below are some notes to the views that follow. Comments are written in the current tense circa 1910. Italics denote comments on subsequent developments.

Page 84
On the way to the docks on the Maumee River we pass downtown. The Lucas County Court House opened in 1897.

Page 85:
The 400 acre Toledo Beach amusement park opened in 1906 on the shore of Lake Erie.

> *(The park's popularity declined rapidly after the interurban trains stopped connecting there in 1927.)*

Lake Erie Park & Casino, a short trolley ride from the city center offers rides, games and vaudeville shows. Opened in 1895, the first casino burned in 1901.

> *(This casino burned in 1910 and was not replaced.)*

The Toledo Yacht Club dates to 1865. The masonry clubhouse, completed in 1908, replaces a frame building destroyed by fire in 1906.

Page 86:
Originally a French settlement founded in 1780, Monroe is located halfway between Toledo and Detroit. This was the hometown of General George Armstrong Custer.

Page 87:
As early as 1876 Captain John Clark had taken Detroit picnickers to Sugar Island on his steamships. Substantial improvements were begun in 1905 when the White Star Line acquired the island. Strategically located, the island park provides a convenient

excursion from Toledo and as a stop for excursionists traveling between Detroit and Toledo. Improvements included a covered dock, a 14,000 square foot dancing pavilion, lunch room, bath houses, boat livery, picnic tables, playground equipment, athletic fields and amusement rides.

(After the White Star Line was dissolved in 1925 the rides were moved to Tashmoo Park. Sugar Island passed to new ownership and continued off-and-on as an excursion destination served by several short run excursion boats. The pavilion burned to the ground in 1954.)

Page 88:
Plans for some sort of tourist attraction on Bois Blanc (Bob-Lo) Island began as early as 1875 when Col. Arthur Rankin, the first owner of the island, announced plans to build a summer hotel and some cottages. The hotel never materialized and the property was late sold to Col. Atkinson and James Randall. In 1888 Randall announced plans for a 100 room Hotel Monte Carlo that never materialized. Finally, in December, 1897, the Detroit, Belle Isle & Windsor Ferry Company purchased 10 acres, made improvements and brought its first boat load of excursionist on June 20, 1898. The island was an immediate success and over the next three years purchased an additional 219 acres, leaving the Randalls with 14 acres. By then the park's improvements included a pavilion, casino, observatory, bath houses, boat houses, lawn ball grounds, bicycle track and lawn tennis courts.

(The 35,000 square foot stone and steel amusement building opened in 1913. It could accommodate 5,000 dancers and at the time may have been the largest dancing pavilion in the world.)

Page 89:
In 1852, shipping magnate Eber Brock Ward established Wyandotte Rolling Mills and Eureka Iron Work, which became America's first Bessemer steel plant. In 1872, he financed the first Great Lakes shipyard created specifically to build metal hulls. In 1877, a few years after the death of E. B. Ward, Michigan's first millionaire, the Detroit Dry Dock Company absorbed the Wyandotte yard. In 1899 the American Shipbuilding Co. absorbed the Detroit Dry Dock Co. In 1905 the Detroit area shipyards accounted for half the tonnage of vessels built on the Great Lakes.

(When the Wyandotte yard closed in 1922 it had produced nearly 300 steel hull ships.)

Building of Fort Wayne was begun in 1843 at a bend in the river where the distance across is the shortest. This site had been the camping ground for troops assembling for the Black Hawk war and the Patriot war (1838 skirmish with Canada) and was also a mobilization camp in 1861.

Page 90:
The Detroit waterfront, at the foot of Woodward.

Page 91:
Dock of the Detroit, Windsor & Belle Isle Ferry Company.

> *(Begun as the Detroit & Windsor Ferry Company in 1873, it ran its last ferry transfer on July 19, 1938.)*

Tashmoo is pulling away from the Line's Griswold Street dock.

The Detroit & Cleveland Steam Navigation Company (D&C Line) dock at the Wayne Hotel Pavilion, foot of 3rd Street. One of its majestic overnight boats is seen cruising down-river.

> *(The City of Detroit steamship is 470 feet long and can carry up to 1,440 passengers in addition to its 230-man crew and 93 automobiles.)*

Page 92:
Campus Martius began as a park where Woodward Avenue, Michigan Avenue and Gratiot Avenue met in the spoked street layout originally designed by Augustus B. Woodward to rebuild the city after the disastrous fire of 1805.

Page 93:
Detroit City Hall
Detroit paid homage to the grandeur of the Second Empire architecture and its own prosperity when work began on the new city hall in 1871. It was dedicated two years later on the 4th of July. The four 14-foot-high statues by Julius Melchers around the cupola are female personifications of the civic virtues: Justice, Art, Industry and Commerce. The second floor niches on the corner pavilions are filled with statues of early French explorers.

> *(The new City-County Building was completed in 1957. The old city hall was demolished in 1961 and the site became Kennedy Square.)*

Wayne County Building
Looking east from the City Hall we see what is unquestionably one of the most sumptuous buildings in Michigan, built in 1902.

This monumental architecture is impressive both for the luxury of its appointments and its architectural sculpture.

Page 94:
The tourist car Yolande meets excursionists at the docks to offer tours along East Jefferson and Woodward Avenue.

Sanders' Palace of Sweets – known as the most beautiful store of its kind in the world and the first to originate the ice cream soda.

Page 95:
This is an era of rapid change in Southeastern Michigan. Factories have been replacing fields and encroaching on city neighborhoods. As much as anything else can, the Ford Motor complex built over the Highland Park RaceTrack is a symbol of the changes taking place in Detroit.

Page 96:
Heading towards Lake St. Clair we pass the Parke Davis & Co. complex on the American side of the river. Originally incorporated in 1867, they began building this riverfront complex in 1872. Chemicals and pharmaceuticals have been a major industry in Detroit since the first salt mines were opened. After New York, Detroit is currently the second largest producer of pharmaceuticals in the nation.

On the Canadian side we pass the Hiram Walker complex. Canadian Whiskey became a major industry here after Michigan's prohibition of the 1890's forced Mr. Walker to move his business to Canada.

Page 97:
The City of Detroit purchased Belle Isle in 1879 with the initial intent of building not only a park connected by a bridge to the U.S. mainland, but also a tunnel to Canada. The ferry dock and pavilion were built in 1884, followed by the first casino in 1886. Major construction began in the late 1880s. The first bridge was built in 1889, but for many years the preferred transportation was by ferry from the Woodward dock. Since 1906 Electric Park, on the mainland next to the bridge, has promoted a "trip through the clouds" on its wooden roller coaster. *Note the Detroit Boat Club beyond the bridge, standing over the water on pilings.*

> *(Electric Park operated until 1928. The wooden bridge was burnt in 1915 and the western end of the island was extended to its present shape in the early 1920's using fill from the trenches dug to lay the last expansion of streetcar rails. At that time the Scott*

Fountain and reflecting pool were added, and dedicated on May 31, 1925. The landscaping of the grounds was completed in 1936.)

In 1904 the nation's first public aquarium was opened and the conservatory from the St. Louis World's Fair was moved to the island.

Page 98:
The island's canals were added in 1893 as part of Frederic Law Olmstead's master plan. The chateau style Skating Pavilion was built in 1894.

(Mr. Olmstead designed New York City's Central Park in 1858. He also contributed to the design of parks and public places in numerous cities including Boston and Philadelphia.)

A wooden Casino was erected in 1886. This was replaced by the Albert Kahn designed brick Italianesque Casino built in 1908.

Page 99:
Belle Isle is home to the Detroit Boat Club and the Detroit Yacht Club. Founded in 1839, the Boat Club is Michigan's oldest social club and the nations oldest boating club. This masonry clubhouse was built in 1902 to replace the 1891 woodframe clubhouse destroyed by fire.

(The DBC continues, but it no longer makes its home on Belle Isle.)

The Detroit Yacht Club, founded in 1868, moved to Belle Isle in 1895 when it took over the clubhouse built by the late Michigan Yacht Club. This clubhouse was built in 1905 to replace one destroyed by fire.

(The current masonry clubhouse was built in 1923.)

Page 100:
The first lighthouse at "Presque Isle" (Windmill Pointe) was built in 1838 and rebuilt in 1866, 1875 and 1891 . At 51 feet high its light is visible for 13 miles.

(The light was automated in 1933 and in the 1970's was removed and relocated to Marine City.)

The Lighthouse Inn opened in 1906. Between 1913 and 1916 it was occupied by the Detroit Motor Boat Club.

(The Veterans Marine Hospital was built here in 1927.)

Beyond the lighthouse lies Grosse Pointe, a long time summer resort that is rapidly growing as a prominent year round community.

Page 101:
Founded in 1884 the Grosse Pointe Club built an impressive clubhouse in 1886. Unsuccessful at first, it closed and reopened as the Grosse Pointe Casino for a number of years, until the County Club of Detroit was organized in 1897. This clubhouse was designed by Albert Kahn and christened on May 30, 1907.

(Later the membership split over boating and golfing priorities, resulting in the creation of a new Grosse Pointe Club commonly known as the "Little Club" and subsequently a new clubhouse replaced the one we see here.)

Farther on is "Lake Terrace," the twin summer homes of John S. Newberry and James McMillan. Originally built in 1875 as mirror images, the original three-story exteriors supported an abundant display of gingerbread detail. In the mid -1880's they were remodeled in the "Shingle Style" architecture.

(Subsequently they were again remodeled and connected with a covered entrance over the common driveway.)

Page 102:
The straight path "Government Channel" opened in 1871. This is a mile shorter than the natural crooked channel (marked by two antebellum lighthouses) it replaced. The dredging created two strips of land that framed the entrance to "The Flats."

(In 1934 the port side strip of land was removed to widen the channel to accommodate a greater volume of commercial shipping. As a commercial shipping route this entrance was abandoned in 1961 when the "Cut-off" channel opened.)

Page 103:
Our first stop is the "Old Club." Founded in 1872, their third clubhouse was built in the shingle-style and has dominated the horizon since 1887.

(Along with the first clubhouse this building was destroyed by fire in 1926 and immediately replaced with the current clubhouse.)

Page 104:

Next we come to the clubhouse built by the Michigan Fishing and Shooting Association in 1889. Originally called the Mervue, it has been succeeded by a number of organizations under names such as the New Mervue, the Mervue Hotel, the New Club and Hotel Muscamoot.

> *(Finally it became the Miller Hotel until it was torn down in the late 1940's and replaced by the Four Winds in the 1960's.)*

Page 105:

In 1884 the Detroit Fishing and Hunting Association was organized and built the largest clubhouse ever constructed at the Flats and named it the Rushmere. Immediately upriver can be seen the Butler cottage. W.A. Butler was the first prominent Detroiter to develop the South Channel when he built his summer home about 1868. The original Rushmere was destroyed by a kitchen fire in 1908 and immediately replaced.

> *(However, in 1923 the club disbanded and the clubhouse was dismantled, with part floated down to the Old Club to be used as helps' quarters and another part floated to Algonac to be used as a boarding house.)*

Page 106:

As the Old Club was a pioneer in providing exclusive society with a resort at the Flats, the Star Island Hotel was the pioneer in providing for the middle classes. Encouraged by the success of their fishing excursions, members of the Star Line group put up a 26-room hotel in 1875. By 1895 it contained 100 rooms and enjoyed the reputation of having the largest dining room in the state, with a seating capacity of 500.

Page 107:

Next we come to the "Marshland," the clubhouse of the Peninsular Fishing and Shooting Club constructed in 1885.

> *(Later it became a public hotel and in October, 1929, the building was destroyed by fire.)*

Page 108:

The Riverside Hotel was opened in 1895.

> *(In 1919 it became the Idle Hour Club. Except for a few brief identity changes it has been known as the Idle Hour to this day.)*

Page 109:

The little Damer Hotel has been operating since the early 1900's.

(Around 1912 it was destroyed by fire and never rebuilt.)

Henry Kehl began developing his resort in the 1870's. When Gustav Trautz acquired the property in 1898 he added a larger pavilion and converted the original to an aviary.

(The resort succeeded to the Foresters and others and today the main building remains as one of the few landmarks of the Flat's Golden Era.)

Page 110:

Joe Bedore first built across the river on the Canadian shore in 1877. In 1881 he was forced to move to the American side, where squatters' rights were not then being challenged. There is no character from the Flats known better than Joe Bedore, "The King of the Flats." His hunting and fishing trips are known the world over.

(This landmark operated until 1960 and was torn down in 1968.)

Page 111:

Beyond Bedore's is the Muir Hotel, the "Last Stop at the Flats." Built in 1890, it has been promoted as a safe place for single women to vacation.

(In 1917 it was put on a barge and taken to Harsens Island where the portico was added and it became a welcomed addition to the Lemke Hotel.)

Next we pass the "Maple Leaf" landing. This prominent dock belongs to a private a community of elegant cottages developed beginning in 1889.

Page 112-113:

Since 1896 an excursion to Tashmoo Park has been a highlight of the summer season for millions. The park's 60 acres including shaded groves and playing fields, were acquired by the White Star Line in 1899. Improvements ultimately included souvenir stands, bathhouse, casino and dance pavilion.

(In 1925 the rides from Sugar Island were moved here. Today the casino and pavilion buildings continue to serve as cover for boat storage. The two-cupola dock shelter collapsed in a September storm in 1953.)

Page 114:
Lemke's Hotel, adjacent to the park.

> (*In 1917 the former Muir Hotel buiding was moved on a barge and added to Lemke's. Later known as the Island House, it was destroyed by fire in 1951.*)

Sans Souci, the island's commercial center since 1890.

> (*The dock's pavilion now covers the Sans Souci Bar.*)

Across the river is Walpole Island home to Chippewa, Ottowa and Potowatami Indians.

Page 115:
The Grande Pointe Hotel opened in 1890 with 60 rooms as the center of a planned sub-division including grand private residences and land reserved for the production of vegetables, fruits, eggs, poultry and dairy products for use at the hotel. In 1902 the hotel's size was doubled to 125 rooms. Next door is the summer home of A.A. Parker, president of the White Star Lines. In 1909 the hotel was destroyed by fire.

Page 116:
We are now approaching Camp Algonac. Since 1905, Russell Island has been leased by the Detroit, Belle Isle & Windsor Ferry Company for a tented resort community to be used by individuals and groups seeking a planned vacation program. As the company's excursion boats are used on its other routes, including Bob-Lo, the White Star Line provides the transportation.

> (*The camp was open only open for a couple of years.*)

Page 117:
The next stop is the City of Algonac, back on the mainland, home of the Chris Craft runabouts. The next stop will be Marine City across from Port Lambton, Ontario.

Page 118:
Approaching the City of St. Clair we come to the Oakland Hotel. The St. Clair Mineral Spring Company established the Oakland Hotel and Hygionama in the 1880's to provide comforts and accommodations superior to any curative mineral springs in America. They boast of having steam elevators for the guests. In addition to the luxurious accommodations and curative mineral baths, amusement and recreation is provided by a dancing hall, clubhouse, bowling alley, billiard parlor, shooting gallery and a boat house supplied with a variety of boats for rowing, sailing and fishing. Following is the city's business district hugging the riverfront.

Page 119:
North of St. Clair we come to the Somerville Hotel and on the Canadian side of the river, opposite the town of Corunna is the Stag Island Resort with the hotels Griffon and Nelson. About 1900 Nelson Mills, a lumberman from Marysville, Michigan, built a pavilion and a dock to attract excursionists. By 1905, accommodations included an elegant dining hall, the hotel Griffon, capable of serving 200 guests, an annex and 21 guest cottages. Mr. Mills' other improvements include a steam operated waterworks, an electric plant, sewage system, bowling alley, tennis courts, pool and long distance telephone connections.

Since then the White Star Line has made four stops daily and a passenger ship from Sarnia, the Hiawatha, makes six trips daily.

(Subsequently, about 1919 the island was acquired by three Detroit fraternal associations; Independent Order of Odd Fellows, Masonic Fraternity, and Knights of Pythias. They proclaimed to have made the world's greatest fraternal resort, platted the land and organized the Fraternal Fellowship Association. The association, made up of the property owners, has managed the island for the benefit of its members ever since.)

Page 120:
Next we approach Lake Huron and our stop at Port Huron. The Hiawatha is just leaving the Black River on its way to Stag Island. Finally, we arrive in Sarnia, Ontario before the ship makes its return.

A Summer Cruise with the White Star Line Squadron

Birds Eye View, Toledo, O.

Steamer "Greyhound" leaving Toledo, O.

GREYHOUND

25387

Dock View. Toledo, O.

Toledo Beach, Toledo, Ohio.

Casino. Toledo, O.

Lagoon Toledo Yachtclub. Toledo, O.

Monroe Yacht Club, Monroe Piers, Monroe, Mich.

Grassy Island Light House, Detroit River.

Dancing Pavilion, At Sugar Island

SUGAR ISLAND PARK
Detroit River

Steamer Greyhound at Sugar Island.

BOB-LO PARK
Bois Blanc Island
Detroit River

Ship Yards, Wyandotte, Mich.

The Old Barracks, Fort Wayne, Detroit, Mich.

9482 WATER FRONT, DETROIT, MICH.

BIRD'S EYE VIEW LOOKING SOUTH OF WOODWARD AVE., DETROIT, MICH.

O'BRIEN & COMPANY GROCERS AND IMPORTING WINE MERCHANTS

Woodward Ave., from River front, Detroit, Mich.

90

Belle Isle Steamer, Woodward Ave. Landing, Detroit, Mich.

1424

COPR. DETROIT PHOTOGRAPHIC CO

6135 OFF FOR A RIVER TRIP.

STEAMER LANDINGS Detroit

D. & C. Line Dock, showing Wayne Pavilion, Detroit, Mich.

220456

PANORAMA OF CAMPUS MARTIUS.
DETROIT, MICH.

Majestic
Building

Woodward
Avenue

Detroit Opera House
Merrill Fountain

Soldiers & Sailors
Monument

CAMPUS MARTIUS

DETROIT CITY HALL
1871 – 1961
WAYNE COUNTY BUILDING
1902 –

1 G   Hurlbut Memorial Gate, Entrance to Water Works Park, Detroit, Mich.

Took this trip Aug 22 - 06

TWO HOUR TOURS
and a stop at
SANDERS' PALACE of SWEETS
originator of the ice cream soda

SANDERS' PALACE OF SWEETS, DETROIT, MICH.

HIGHLAND PARK CLUB,

A CORNER of HIGHLAND PARK
before
&
after 1908

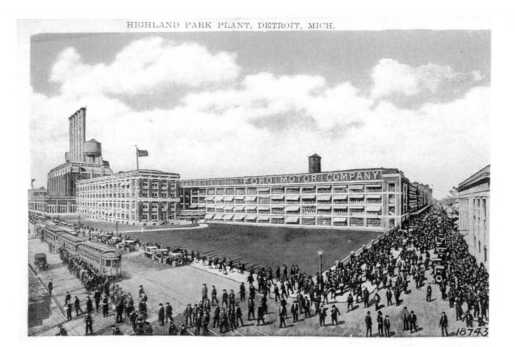

HIGHLAND PARK PLANT, DETROIT, MICH.

FORD MOTOR COMPANY

Birdseye View of Parke Davis & Co., of Detroit, Mich., from Detroit River.

PARK DAVIS & CO., U.S.A.
Facing
HIRAM WALKER, Ltd., Canada

WALKERVILLE, ONTARIO, CANADA. THE HOME OF "CANADIAN CLUB" WHISKY.

DISTILLERY OFFICES, MALT HOUSES AND GRAIN ELEVATOR.

Belle Isle, as seen from an Aeroplane, Detroit, Mich.

"AEROPLANE PHOTO BY COURTESY OF THE DETROIT NEWS."   217932

BELLE ISLE LANDING
&
THE ISLAND TOURIST BUS

Sight Seeing Car
at Aquarium,
Belle Isle,
Detroit, Mich.

Pavilion, Belle Isle, Detroit, Mich.

CASINO, BELLE ISLE PARK, DETROIT, MICH. 6212

Detroit Boat Club, Belle Isle, Detroit, Mich.

Detroit Yacht Club, Detroit, Mich.

1327

13335 WINDMILL POINTE, LAKE STE. CLAIRE.

LIGHTHOUSE & INN
at
Windmill Pointe

Aeroplane View of Country Club, Boat Landing and Lighthouse, Detroit, Mich.

"AEROPLANE PHOTO BY COURTESY OF THE DETROIT NEWS"   217942

New Country Club, Grosse Pointe—Suburb of Detroit, Mich.

Drive on Lake Front; Grosse Point.

Detroit Mich.

No. 5437 Published by The Detroit News Company Detroit Mich., Leipzig, Dresden.

Summer Residences, Grosse Pointe.

Detroit, Mich.

101

10018. STE. CLAIRE SHIP CANAL, LOWER ENTRANCE.

Imagine your Ma out in a row boat Tom.

Ever More.

ENTERING THE FLATS
through the
"Government Channel"

5495   STR. "TASHMOO" ENTERING SAINTE CLAIRE SHIP CANAL.   DETROIT PUBLISHING CO.

COPR. DETROIT PUBLISHING CO.

13887 THE VENICE OF AMERICA, STE. CLAIRE FLATS, MICH.

71958 THE "OLD CLUB", STE. CLAIRE FLATS, MICH.

COPR. DETROIT PUBLISHING CO.

10050. OLD CLUB, STE. CLAIRE FLATS, MICH.   A SECTION OF OUR AMERICAN VENICE.

COPYRIGHT 1906 BY DETROIT PUBLISHING CO.

Mervue Club, St. Clair Flats, Mich.

THE New Mervue
ST. CLAIR FLATS

"Rushmere" St. Clair Flats, Mich.

10015. RUSHMERE CLUB STE. CLAIRE FLATS. MICH.

Helo Norman from Ed.

Along the "Flats", Lake St. Clair

6400   STAR ISLAND HOUSE, STE. CLAIRE FLATS, MICH.

"Marshland" St. Clair Flats, Mich.

13866 MARSHLAND, STE. CLAIRE FLATS, MICH.

RIVERSIDE HOTEL, ST. CLAIR FLATS, MICH.

G.L. 3823B

12062. COTTAGES AT STE. CLAIRE FLATS, MICH.

Detroit, Mich.

"The Damer" St. Clair Flats, Mich.

Feb. 26 - 1907

TRAUTZ HOTEL, St. Clair Flats, Mich.

Aug 12, 05 *have thought about you all day*

Joe Bedores Hotel; St. Claire Flats. Detroit, Mich.

Dear Ethel this is where we are spending the day Expect to Detroit home tomorrow hope you got to Benton

No. 1111   Published by The Detroit News Company, Detroit, Mich.-Leipzig-Berlin *Harbor alright. Mother*

9302   JOE BEDORE'S HOTEL, STE. CLAIRE FLATS, MICH.

LEMKE'S HOTEL AND SUMMER RESORT ADJOINING TASHMOO PARK, HARSEN'S ISLAND, MICH.

Maple Leaf, St. Clair Flats, Mich.

Dear Lou,— I hope we will see you on Sunday. I will be O.K. Tell George to bring his piano — Gert. (not to forget his music roll — $)

Landing, Tashmoo Park, St. Clair Flats.

A1642

Bathing at Tashmoo Park, St. Clair Flats, Mich.

Dancing Pavilion, Tashmoo Park, St. Clair River, Mich.

INDIAN SOUVENIR STANDS, TASHMOO PARK, ST. CLAIR FLATS.

Pavilion Tashmoo Park, St. Clair River. Detroit, Mich.

113

Lemke's St. Clair Flats.

Sans Souci, St. Clair Flats, Mich.

2045   WALPOLE ISLAND   PESHA PHOTO

10014. GRANDE POINTE HOTEL, STE. CLAIRE RIVER, MICH.

Grande Pointe Hotel, St. Clair Flats.

Every body's happy, with love Vinnie

Lula

We go here to-night & Verne

CAMP ALGONAC.

Camp Algonac, Algonac, Mich.

White Star Line Landing, Algonac, St. Clair River, Mich.

220470

Marine City, Mich., Steamer Tashmoo at Dock.

Lake Front, St. Clair, Mich.

3828

River Front, St. Clair, Mich.

SOMERVILLE HOTEL, ST. CLAIR, MICH.

10013. STAG ISLAND CASINO. NEAR PORT HURON. MICH.

Hotels Griffon and Nelson, Stag Island,
Marysville, Mich.

119

9300. BLACK RIVER, PORT HURON, MICH.

Oct. 3, 1906. *All aboard for Canada*
Your loving Dan

COPYRIGHT 1905 BY DETROIT PUBLISHING

COPYRIGHT, 1905, BY DETROIT PUBLISHING CO.

11862 STEAMERS AT DOCK, PORT HURON.

Along the Docks at Sarnia, Canada.

120

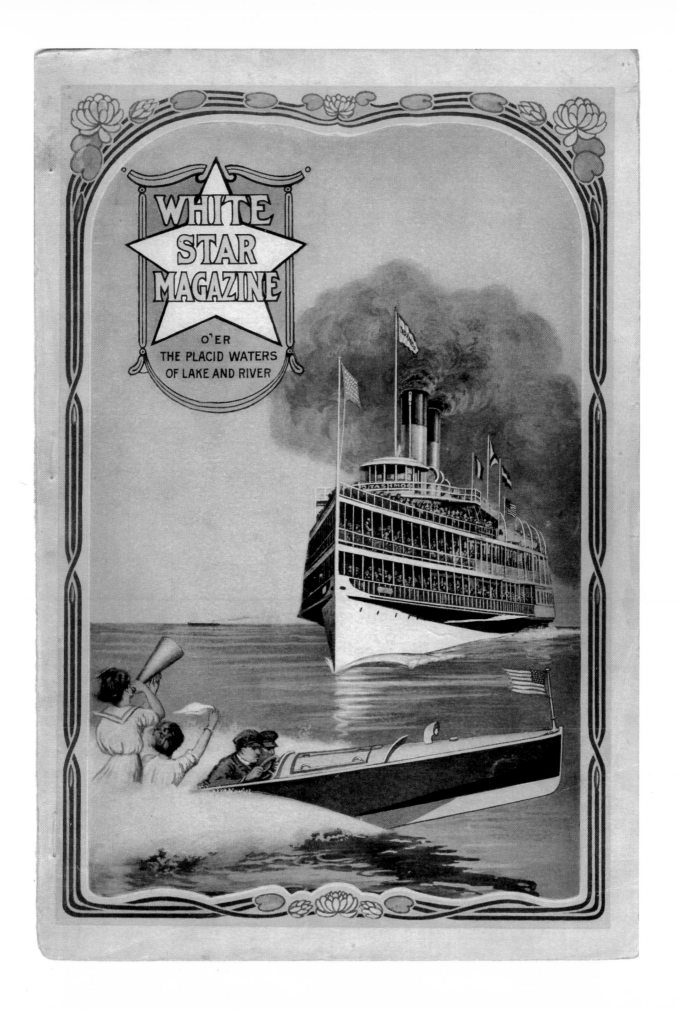

WHITE STAR MAGAZINE

O'ER
THE PLACID WATERS
OF LAKE AND RIVER

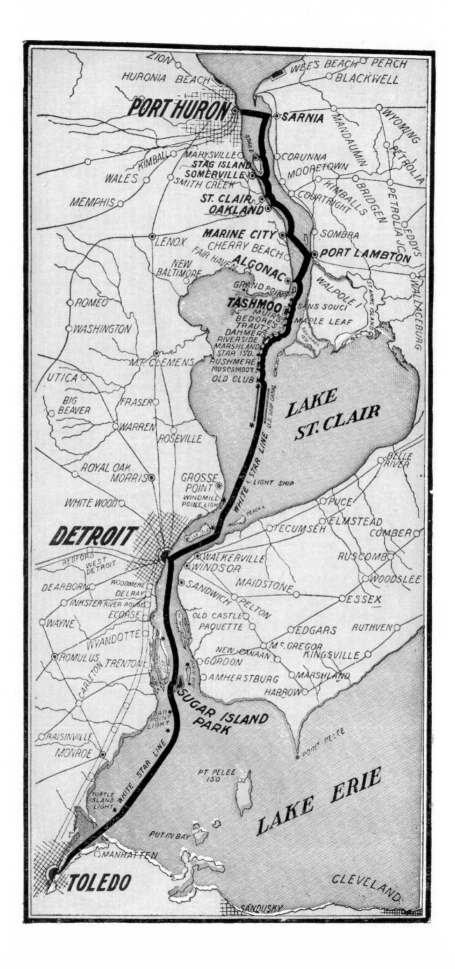

The following text originally appeared in the 1906 White Star Magazine, an annual publication of the White Star Line Company. Opinions expressed represent the unedited bias of a bygone era.

The Offerings of the White Star Line to a Recreation Seeking Public

This whirling world's a great round globe,
Which Nature's giv'n to man
Within its shell you'll pleasures find;
Enjoy them if you can.
— Ellen Erg.

THE SOLITARY GRANDEUR of the wilds appeal to few; the many enjoy the bustling activities of the channels of trade, and commercial and industrial centers. It is the desire of the average citizen to live in touch with other human beings.

Luckily for social and industrial progress, the hermit is the exception, while the living soul seeking companionship is the rule. Thus, while one hides away to the solitude for his recreation, a thousand hurry to where they can join with others in pursuing pleasure during summer vacation.

Yet, the charms of nature are not to be lightly considered. They have their proper places in the economy of the universe, and the human being is indeed akin to a brute if he can look on sky and water—drifting clouds and rippling waves—on primeval forests with their towering and straight-limbed monarchs, and on the embowered banks of meandering streams, without having his soul stirred within him.

Whether a lover of the hill or dale, of land or water, the truly wise man takes his vacation in the society of his equals. Draughts at the health-giving fount of Nature are always deeper, purer and better when enjoyed with congenial companions.

The route of the White Star Line between Toledo, Detroit, and Port Huron, is a wonderful combination of Man's art and Nature's handiwork. The Arts of Man predominate, yet there is enough of Nature to satisfy even the most romantically inclined. The three large cities on the route have, with their suburbs,

123

the better part of a million inhabitants, and it is safe to say that five hundred thousand more live within sight, and certainly within sound, of the whistles of the Tashmoo, the Greyhound, the City of Toledo, and the Owana, comprising the company's fleet of swiftly propelled and elegantly furnished steamers.

While little of the Great Lakes themselves are covered on the White Star Line route, still the waters of Lake Erie can be enjoyed, and Lake Huron's cool breezes can be felt and its broad bosom seen when the boats arrive at their northern terminus.

The Maumee River, with its coal and iron docks; Lake Erie, with a touch of history connected with Put-in-Bay, the scene of Perry's famous naval victory in the war of 1812: the Detroit River, twenty-five miles long, and offering a great variety of scenery; Lake St. Clair, in the midst of which can be found Michigan's Little Venice, a city set in the waters and a unique summer resort: the St. Clair River with its Indian Reservation, its islands and its enterprising cities and villages; and Detroit, the great Metropolis of Michigan, midway between termini of the route—these are some of the things to be enjoyed on the White Star Line boats—things historic, romantic, commercial, and social.

In searching for recreation, and enjoyment then, there can be nothing better found anywhere than is offered by the White Star Line. There has never been any serious accident on the route, the most that has occurred is an occasional delay from causes beyond human foresight; but on steam or streetcars, autos or omnibuses, connections are liable to be missed. This is the very worst that has happened on this route, and that not often. No passenger has been lost; no one has been maimed or crippled.

With these few remarks by way of introduction, the reader is earnestly requested to read the following pages, to the end, that he may become familiar with at least some of the interesting objects to be seen in a day's outing on the White Star Line steamers.

Toledo a Busy Mart

"Generous commerce binds the round of Nations
In a golden chain"
-Thomson

TOLEDO IS OHIO'S THIRD METROPOLIS. Taking the city proper with its suburbs, close on to 200,000 people are engaged in its many activities, the thousand or so factories and commercial houses employing 40,000 men and women and the usual quota of children. It is a shipping point of more than ordinary importance because of its location at the head of Lake Erie and the fourteen great railroad lines touching it.

Besides being a great shipping point, Toledo is also a beautiful residence city, with asphalt streets, stone sidewalks, modern residences, velvety lawns and well-shaded avenues. In the west and northwest portions there has been an evolution from vacant fields to beautiful environments. The City is well officered, its thoroughfares are clean, and public-spirited citizens with plenty of civic pride watch over the financial, social and industrial interests of the people.

The landing dock of the White Star Line is at the foot of Adams Street. From this point, the very center of the city, the depots of the various railroads can be easily reached. The Greyhound leaves the dock at 8:30 each morning (SUNDAYS at 9 o'clock) during the season of navigation, and Toledo being several miles from the lake on the Maumee river, at the very beginning of the trip passengers are given fascinating views of the city's busy marts of iron and coal docks, of factories and manufacturing plants with their tall chimneys from which columns of more or less smoke is ascending, and of the fine driveways, footpaths, fountains, foliage and flowers of Riverside Park, as well as being in close touch with the Maumee's teeming traffic.

On the east bank of the Maumee River lies Presque Isle, with its many boat and clubhouses, and where the voices of happy, laughing children are always to be heard. Here the Maumee's channel is broader and deeper, and the captain takes advantage of this fact to put on more steam, when the pulsating engines quickly carries the steamer into the clearer water of the lake.

A first view of any large body of water is always interesting, and a sight of Lake Erie is no exception to this rule. There is buoyancy to the steamer when it strikes deep water, and the effect is felt by every person on board. Off to the north are trails of smoke from funnels of numerous freighters towing consorts, while low on the horizon to the east are Put-in-Bay and the other famous islands, noted not alone for their graperies, but also for the historic fact that it was here that Commandore Perry won his victory, which he announced in the famous phrase: "We have met the enemy and they are ours."

The ozone of Lake Erie adds to the health giving value of this trip. Ozone is exhilarating, enriching the blood, sending it coursing through the arteries and veins, and increasing the power of the pulsations. It is both health and color giving. Rich blood will do more for "pale people" than all the plain, tinted, or varicolored pills in the world.

In fact, one day's outing on the White Star Line route is sufficient to remove all paleness and a week of it will help restore strength and annihilate illness. Lake breezes are no friend to the "White Plague."

As the Greyhound plows her way through the limpid green waters, Ohio fades away and Michigan scenery begins to come into view. Back on the River Raisin, with its lotus beds, lies Monroe and curling smoke or dust clouds indicate the presence of hamlets and villages with their minor industrial activities. It is to be remembered during the early part of the nineteenth century these same shores where the favorite stamping grounds of Indians. Their tepees have disappeared, their homes have crumpled to dust, but the history of their lives recorded by the early Jesuits still remain with us.

Sugar Island Park

Go, get your basket full of grub;
Hitch on Maria; come along, bub
                              -O.R. Iginal.

NOW THE YAWNING MOUTH OF THE DETROIT RIVER comes into view. Here amidst a cluster of islands is to be seen besides Bois Blanc and Hickory, Sugar Islands with its beautifully curved shores, its natural and shady groves and its high and dry ground. Sugar Island, even more than the mainland was once a favorite resort of the Indians. Their wigwams and bark canoes are now only a memory, but historians and romancists have recounted in prose and verse the loves and hates, the friendship and treachery of the Red Men of this region. Here they lived, loved and were happy. They pursued the timid deer, they moored their canoes in the little rush-hidden bays and fished and when war was proclaimed against some neighboring or even distant tribe, it was from the shelter of these same islands that the painted savages went forth: but before going they danced their war dances and sang their war songs. Often returning defeated, a little remnant would chant the story of their failure.

But what a change has taken place! On all sides are lighthouses or range lights, and the commerce of the Great Lakes passes by Sugar Island with hardly a thought of the past. Instead of wigwams, are music and dancing pavilions, swings, rest houses, refreshment booths and baseball and picnic grounds. The arts of man for amusement of man have added to the natural beauties of the place, and swift sailing yachts and still swifter gasoline launches usurp the place once occupied by bark canoes.

Nature sings her most melodious songs where, as in Sugar Island Park, sky and land and water are in right proportions.

Sugar Island is now the property of the White Star Line, and the thirty and more acres have been converted into a beautiful pleasure park for the private and exclusive use of its patrons. That no more suitable spot could be chosen for the purpose, is the unanimous opinion of all who have seen it since upwards of $30,000 have been expended on a covered wharf; on a dancing pavilion 100 x 140, and thus containing 14,000 square feet of dancing surface, and where an orchestra furnishes music free to dancing parties; on a parlor; on a lunch room, where hot coffee, sandwiches and other refreshments can be had at reasonable prices (no liquors permitted on the Island Park): and on bath houses for bathers where they can enjoy the clear, cool waters of the Detroit River.

These buildings, in the event of a rainstorm, will comfortably shelter four thousand people, so that there is never any necessity for getting wet.

Sugar Island Park is nearly surrounded with sandy beach and here young and old have the opportunity of wading or swimming. Being well sheltered, the limpid waters lap the sloping banks with hardly a ripple save at the further end, where the wind is in the right direction, when the waves rolling in from Lake Erie and breaking on the beach, add a new fascination to this delightful spot.

In the park, besides the buildings mentioned, are baseball diamonds, sprinting tracks, swings, merry-go-rounds, rustic benches, tables and every modern convenience for picnicking, all free to patrons.

A boat livery is at hand for those who desire to spend a part of time on the water, and a staunch steam yacht is always ready for those who would like to make an excursion to Amherstburg, Canada, or other nearby points. Everything possible that could be thought of has been provided for the comfort and enjoyment of men, women, and children.

Sugar Island Park is for the exclusive use of church, Sunday school, society, club, family and picnic excursions leaving Toledo every morning at 8:30 o'clock, (Sundays at 9:00), on the magnificent steel steamer Greyhound, built expressly for the people of Ohio in 1902. The round trip costs fifty cents for adults and twenty-five cents for children between five and twelve years of age (children under five free). The return trip leaves the island at 5:10 p.m., (Sundays at 6:10 p.m.), reaching Toledo two and a half hours later.

Speeding Through the Detroit River

"From bubbling springs beyond the horizon's rim
This river has its birth.
Now on its broad bosom ran float
A world's commerce."

- L. Le Nerg

AT THE MOUTH OF THE DETROIT RIVER the Greyhound uses the American channel, passing between Sugar and Hickory Islands. All other steam vessels hug the Canadian shore in pursuing their way north. There are really two channels in the lower reaches of the Detroit River, it is the one along the Canadian shore that has been widened and deepened in the effort to make the famous Limekiln Crossing-a ledge of rocks at the bottom of the river-have at least twenty feet of depth of water over its sharp edges and big boulders under all conditions of weather and all directions of the wind.

The other channel runs between Grosse Isle and the American shore. It has a good depth of water, but to make it navigable for the large, heavy laden freight craft now being used in lake commerce, not a little blasting and dredging would be necessary. This has often been advocated by patriotic Americans who want to have all the river improvements on Uncle Sam's premises. However, the channel has uses, it being principally used by the steamers plying between Detroit and the shore points to Trenton.

The Canadian side of the Detroit River is pastoral looking. For many years French Canadians have tilled the soil of their little farms, raising early vegetables and grapes for the Detroit and Windsor markets. They have been content to live as their fathers and grandfathers lived, and many of their little houses show no improvement over those built a century ago. Indeed, some of them are weatherworn mementos of an unprogressive and unambitious ancestry.

But there are also on the Canadian side evidences of wealth and taste, especially as Detroit is neared. Sandwich, to be sure, which is one of the oldest settlements in Upper Canada, is quaint and ancient looking with its cathedral and jail, its courthouse and convent. Still after all, there are plenty of modern residences lining the northeast bank of the river, some owned by Americans and some by Canadians.

The American side of the Detroit River, between Trenton and Detroit, has a commercial look. The land is low and marshy, and numerous derricks rear their heads above the surrounding country. Back a little way are to be seen huge buildings with tall chimneys. Under all this region is a great bed of salt and these derricks are salt wells, from which are pumped the brine, later to be manufactured into various articles of commerce.

Already the greater part of 10,000 men are employed in this work, representing a population of from 30,000 to 50,000 people living by this one industry alone. And it has only begun. Back a little way from the river a shaft is being sunk through the nine hundred feet of solid rock and overlapping the four hundred foot thick salt bed, and it is expected that when completed this new way of getting the salt to the surface will add still greater impetus to the industry.

Among the largest of the plants using brine as a raw material is the Solvay Process Co., at the mouth of the River Rouge, its immense iron crane, and its huge chimney 260 feet high, being landmarks of great significance and importance, for from the tops of the chimney are sent wireless messages to vessels on the lakes, keeping them in touch with their owners on shore.

A short distance back, on the Rouge, is the Michigan Carbon Works, and a little farther down the Detroit River are great shipbuilding plants from which 500 and 550 footers are now being turned out, regular leviathans each carrying 10,000 or 12,000 tons of freight at one load.

It is these things that give the flavor of commercialism to the American shore of the Detroit River. They tell of labor and capital united and working harmoniously in the production of wealth, of the thrift and enterprise, of daring industrial ventures and of faith in the future of Detroit and of the Republic.

Yet there is also sentiment on the American side of the river, for just east of Solvay Process Co.'s works and a short distance past the plant of the Edison Electric Light Co. can be seen the Flag of the Union-Old Glory-Floating from its flagstaff above Fort Wayne.

Fort Wayne is an old style fortification guarding the southern river approaches to Detroit. The quarters for the men are in more or less modern brick buildings, while in a maple grove and in view from the deck of the Greyhound are the officers houses-separate residences-fronting a great sloping lawn reaching to the river margin. The foot is edged in by a moat and is reached by subterranean passageways. The whole is more picturesque than formidable and it is feared that a shot or two from a modern 12-inch gun would make sad havoc with these ancient defenses. There are always a company or two of regulars doing duty at Fort Wayne, for it is a healthy location and much desired for a resting place by troops returning from the enervating climate of the Philippine Islands.

The ride from Sugar Island Park to Detroit, which comes into view, is an hour well spent. Past the great coal docks the Greyhound has sped, past freight, ferry slips and elevators, past copper and iron works belching out volumes of black smoke: and now she turns toward shore and with ever decreasing speed at last gently reaches her dock at the foot of Griswold Street, only five minutes walk from the city hall from which the main avenues of the metropolis radiate like spokes from the hub of a wheel.

Detroit River is a little less than a mile wide. It is from 40 to 80 feet in depth, with a three or four mile current, according to the direction of the wind. The water is clear, and from brim to brim there is a commercial activity that is fascinating, for on an average a freighter passes each seven minutes, to make no mention of the ferry boats and pleasure craft taking advantage of this, one of the world's safest harbors.

But let us hasten to disembark, for there has now come the opportunity to catch glimpses of one of the most unique and remarkable cities in America-a city of 400,000 inhabitants representing all nations, with a history dating back over two hundred years and with an industrial future already mapped out that is sure to place it in the forefront of America's commercial centers.

Beautiful, Romantic, and Industrial Detroit

"A tale of a beautiful city.
Where the arts of peace have brought
Prosperity and happiness."
-Ellen Fry

TAKE IT ALL IN ALL, Detroit is the most beautiful city on the American continent. Here Art and Nature vie with each other in providing beautiful effects. It is laid out in such a way that the center cannot shift, its broad avenues converging to one point. The land rises gradually from the riverbank giving perfect drainage, and many streets have from two to four rows of shade trees. There are big and little parks scattered north, east and west, and a great broad boulevard, fourteen miles long and two hundred feet wide, encircles the entire city.

Many miles of streets are asphalted, many more miles are paved with brick and cedar blocks on a concrete foundation, and the boulevards are macadamized and daily dampened to lay the dust. Along these thoroughfares speed many hundreds of automobiles, both for pleasure and for business, while the street car service-some lines carrying passengers eleven miles for three cents-is the cheapest and as good, if not better, than can be found anywhere else.

In the very center of Detroit is the Campus Martius, with its Soldier's Monument and the Palmer Marble Fountain. A little north, less than five minutes walk, is Grand Circus Park, beautifully shaded, adorned with fountains and containing a fine bronze monument to the late Governor Pringree. Still further along, at the northern terminus of the Woodward avenue car line, six miles out, and reached at a cost of five cents, is Palmer Park, containing lakes and fountains, winding roadways and embowered footpaths, and, besides, a log home in the style of a century ago. This log house is divided by a hall through the middle, with kitchen on one side and living room on the other. Everything is old fashioned and gives the sightseer a good idea of how the western fathers of the Republic lived.

To fail to visit Belle Isle, the city's Island Park, which can be reached by boat every twenty minutes, or by street car out Jefferson avenue every five minutes, is to miss the most brilliant gem of all the jewels in Detroit's diadem of beautiful scenes. The park contains about seven hundred acres, and was originally bought by the city in 1879 for $200,000. Since that time various commissions have been in charge and besides spending a million dollars in its maintenance, have expended over a million more in its beautification and adornment. The low spots have been dug out and made into lakes, and these in turn are connected by canals which meander in and out, all the while disclosing new beauties in the scenery to those who are taking a boat or canoe ride.

Rustic and stone bridges have been flung over these canals, and driveways and footpaths penetrate the northern part of the island which has been left, except for draining, in a state of nature. Ball, cricket, and tennis grounds have been laid out: a commodious greenhouse and a fine aquarium have been built and filled with plants and fishes; a bath, bathing suits, boats and boat houses, shelters and band stands, and merry-go rounds, swings and teeters are to be found at convenient points. Besides there are drinking fountains, parks and enclosures for other wild animals are always on view, and, as is natural, attract great crowds of sightseers.

Nowhere on the Island can there be seen the sign "Keep off the Grass." People can lie, sit, or walk on the green sward as please their fancy. They can lunch wherever they please, tables and benches being scattered throughout the island in great profusion. About the only thing visitors are not allowed to do is pick the flowers or break the shrubbery. To permit this would be to deprive others of the pleasure of seeing them bud and blossom.

A half-mile-long bridge connects Belle Isle with mainland. The bridge is no obstruction to navigation, the main channel being on the other side of the island. But it has a commodious draw, which is opened, as occasion requires.

If romance is wanted, then Detroit can supply it in abundance. First located by De la Mothe Cadillac in 1701, it almost immediately became an important trading post, where the wares of civilization were exchanged for fur pelts, particularly beaver skins. It flew the French, then the British, then the American flags. Indian wars swept around its fort and Indian massacres were perpetrated at its very threshold. It was Detroit the Gen. Hull ignominiously surrendered, and it was Chief Pontiac who made a last desperate effort, by uniting all the Indian tribes of the region, to capture the town and wipe the white men off the face of the earth.

Detroit triumphed over all the vicissitudes of its early existence, and came through triumphant. Gradually its borders were widened and when, in 1805 a disastrous fire swept the center of town and removed every landmark, Congress gave its Governor and judges authority to lay it out as suited their pleasure, only prescribing that all the previous landowners should be fairly dealt with in the new distribution.

This accounts for the fact that the center of the city is after the plan adopted at Washington, and still earlier at Versailles, France, once home of French royalty. One of the Judges had been to France, and it struck him that here was the opportunity to lay out an American city in the very best way possible. Unfortunately, the complete plan was never followed, else Detroit, charming as it is would today be still more beautiful. However there was enough of the general plan followed to make its laying out unique, so that travelers from Europe are apt to remark the resemblance of Detroit to old world views where landscape artists and architects have united in giving grace and beauty to such commonplace objects as streets, parks and avenues.

Aside from being noted as the most beautiful and best-governed city in America, Detroit has every reason to be more than proud of her remarkable industrial development.

When Chevalier Cadillac planted the tricolor of France and founded the settlement, which developed into the beautiful City of, the Straits he probably had not the remotest idea that it was destined to grow into a vast commercial center.

But the city's commanding position on the chain of lakes, together with the natural beauty of its many miles of water front, have combined to attract the manufacturer, the investor, and the pleasure seeker in ever increasing numbers.

Like other cosmopolitan cities it has its "sky scrapers," its fine hotels, built or in process of building, its palatial residences and magnificent churches, its art museum, and splendid schools and colleges. But, unlike most other commercial cities, it has a large number of the greatest industrial establishments in the world.

Fifteen hundred factories give employment to 100,000 mechanics, clerks and laborers. It manufactures more automobiles than any other commercial center in the world. It has the largest drug manufacturing plant in the world. It has the largest stove foundries in the world. Its wire cloth factory is the most extensive in the world. It is the greatest paint and varnish center. One special factory alone has filled an order for 10,000 go-carts for London, Eng., from whence they have been distributed all over Europe. Its immense shipyards last year turned out more big steamships built for carrying the traffic of the Great Lakes, than those of any other fresh water port.

For many years Detroit-built steam yachts, gasoline launches, motor boats and row boats have been shipped by land and sea to all parts of the world, so that in addition to her many other industries, Detroit is now undoubtedly the greatest pleasure-boat building center of the continent.

Its brass and copper industries exceed in their united output any other city in the world. Its fur trade is an exceedingly important part of the fur trade of the country. It is the center of the overall trade of America, and its two great pin factories are important factors in the pin trade. Pin, pills and pharmaceutical preparations, overalls, autos, stoves, ships and pleasure craft, no wonder Detroit commands attention in the world of trade and commerce, and no wonder its name is a valuable trade-mark and a synonym for good goods. It may seem farfetched, but it is true, nevertheless, that where manufacturers and operators have congenial environments and work amidst charming scenes, the dead raw materials in their hands become in time a part of their lives, and take on some of the attributes of their surroundings. Beauty seldom exists in slums. A factory in the center of green plants, shrubbery and flowerbeds can always find market for its wares, because its output is better than the output of competitors not so happily situated.

Detroit factories in the main contain all the modern conveniences. They are light and airy, and some of them models of elegance, and the proprietors have made them still more acceptable as places of employment by providing restaurants run at cost, rest and bath rooms, and even gymnasiums and meeting halls for the fraternal and social organizations with which their employees may be connected. It is these things that help make the City of the Straits such a splendid place in which to earn a living.

But delightful as is the subject, one must not linger too long in beautiful Detroit. The voyage is not half completed, and the fascination of Michigan's Little Venice, a city set in the waters of the St. Clair River, are still to be experienced.

Lake St. Clair and America's Venice

"Haste! Make haste! and catch the Tashmoo
As she sails upon the waters
Towards the Venice of the Inlands.
Towards the Island of the Walpoles.
Towards the City of the Hurons.

-John S. Owen

EVERY MORNING at 8:30 o'clock (Sunday at 9:00,) and every afternoon at 2:30, (and 3:30 o'clock, except Sunday) during the season, the Tashmoo, City of Toledo, and Owana leave the White Star Line dock at the foot of Griswold street for their trips to St. Clair Flats, Tashmoo Park and the stopping places on the St. Clair River. Altogether, there are twenty four landings, two of them on the Canadian side of the border.

The boat promptly leaves the dock on time, and, gliding out into the stream, quickly passes on the American side the Public Lighting and Detroit United Railway tall chimmeyed power houses, the Michigan and Detroit Stove Foundries, Park, Davis & Co. great drug and bacteriological establishments, the Queen Anne Soap Works and Belle Isle. On the Canadian side can be seen Windsor, Walkerville, with its great distillery, and Peche Island, once the summer resort of Pontiac, chief of the once powerful tribe of Ottwa Indians. Here he would live through the hot months with his four wives, sleeping away the time, or engaged in lying plans to punish his enemies. At such times, the island was sacred ground, to visit, which was to invite disaster, if not death. Now Peche Isle is the private summer resort of the Walker family.

Just beyond Peche Isle, but to the left, is Windmill Point, from whence the course to the government canal, twenty miles away, is straight as can be. The channel is 800 feet wide, and twenty or more feet deep and many buoys mark its limits. Half way between Windmill Point and the "piers," the local name for the government canal, a lightship serves as a point of observation by day and a beacon by night. The wooden shores of Lake St. Clair are still to be seen on the left, the foliage, both hiding and revealing the village of Grosse Point farms, containing the costly summer residences of Detroit millionaires.

On the lakes, there is a procession of freighters- "huge forms with breath of steam"- growing larger in size and increasing in number each year. As its boats keep to comparatively narrow channel, tourists have close views of these great vessels, some of 12,000 tons freight capacity and with thirty or more hatchways, and their varieties and peculiarities become an interesting study.

It is only a short run of an hour and forty minutes across Lake St. Clair the willow-clad governmental canal, which is a mile and a quarter long, and dug and spilled to straighten the channel and shorten the route. Now another channel is being excavated alongside the first one, and it is interesting to watch the big dredges sucking up the bottom of the channel and shooting it through long jointed pipes onto islands half a mile distant.

It is at the piers that St. Clair Flats- America's Venice- begins, and it is the commencement of the journey through a wonderland of natural and artificial beauties. The Flats is a delta formed by the silt dropping to the bottom of the lake at the mouth of the St. Clair River, and gradually filling up the channel until the deposits reached the surface. Then flotsam began to catch on the bars, and after a while there was land on which hunting and fishing boxes could be built. There was only one or two of these on the whole Flats fifty years ago, but with the fame of the spot for fishing and duck shooting rapidly spread, and, keeping pace with the population of Detroit and Michigan, first modest cottages and then clubhouses and hotels were erected, until today five thousand people can be fed and housed in America's Venice in short notice.

Nowhere else can there be found such a summer resort. The houses are built upon piles driven in the silt, and often there is running water all around, the boats being moored to the very doorsteps. In the river and cuts are deep pools and swift currents, the homes of the gamy bass or lively perch. Quantities of pickerel and pike are also caught here. There are everywhere facilities for bathing and boating, and though there is not much land, little is needed where there are so many other things to interest and amuse.

This "city in the waters" with its liquid streets and roadways, has no gloomy antiquities or crumbling marbles like ancient Venice, but is sweet and fresh with summer homes. Here the clamor, and dust, and heat of the town is forgotten, for nature is kind to sweltering humanity when sweltering humanity has the sense to come, the cool breezes from the lakes tempering the atmosphere and making living a delight.

So the Old Club and the Rushmere, Mervue, Star Island and Joe Bedores's Marshland and the Riverside, Damer's and Trautz's (the German Village), and Muir's Landing, all stopping places on the Flats, have become centers around which cluster cottages, each ministering to its particular class of patrons. Some are hotels, some are clubhouses, and the tourist will be made welcome at any of them, though club rules will have to be stretched at times, to accommodate those who are not members.

The St. Clair River divides itself into three channels through the Flats- North, Middle and South Channels- but commerce has chosen the South Channel for its main thoroughfare and it is this that the White Star also uses. It winds and turns, one side being the United States and the other Canada, and finally straightening its course to the northwest, Tashmoo Park soon comes into view.

Tashmoo Park

When your brains and hands are weary,
When you need a jolly lark,
Come with song and laughter cheery,
Come and dance at Tashmoo Park.

M. McN. J.

TASHMOO PARK is a growth. Its sixty acres, the property of the White Star Line, at first consisting of nothing but a natural grove of trees, has been beautified until it is an ideal pleasure spot. In front is the noble St. Clair River with its splendid bathing beach, on which is located bathhouses and covered dock. Running back from the river is a broad avenue lined with trees and leading to a large shelter and dancing hall. Here too, are refreshment stands, and close by swings and teeters, benches and lunch tables. The park also contains baseball diamonds, cinder paths for running races and other accommodations for athletic sports. The grove furnishes superb shelter from the sun, and underneath the trees' branches, there is room for thousands to picnic. Is mother a weary? Are children tired from the excess of romping pleasures? Then they can go to the "rest room," where if wanted, a nap may be taken and strength renewed for other experiences. Meanwhile the orchestra furnishes music, free, for those who desire to dance, and Indians from Walpole Island, which is an Indian reservation under the control of the Canadian government, come down in their boats and sell baskets, moccasins, bows and arrows, and other evidences of their handiwork.

Sometimes an Indian chief, filled with the ambition of his forefathers and the vanities of his race will dress in buckskin garments, decorate himself with paint and feathers, and visit the park, strutting around to be admired. Little children are sometimes afraid, but this soon wears off, and it is not an uncommon sight to see a "brave" leading a child in each hand, visit a refreshment stand and become for the moment a "civilized" savage. Many a good string of fish has been caught right off the Tashmoo dock, and the boys who have learned wisdom from experience do not neglect to bring with them line, sinker, hooks, and bait, and add to the pleasures of the trip by hauling in a dozen or so of perch or pickerel. One can only fish by hook and line at the Flats, as the Michigan legislature has made it a state preserve, under the control of the game and fish warden. On the Canadian side a license, costing $5.00 is necessary before one can legally fish. These precautions help to keep the Flats good fishing grounds.

Up to this point, the tourist will notice that only the American side of the Flats is built upon. On the Canadian side for several miles are only to be seen two houses. Some have accounted for this as "Yankee enterprise" and " Canadian unprogressiveness". These have another guess coming. The real reason is that the Canadian side, clear up to Algonac, is an Indian reservation. Here several scores of Indians and half breeds live on their annuities, supplemented by a little agriculture and a little fishing and hunting, and none but Indians, except by their permission are allowed on the reservation. The Canadian government enforces this law rigidly, and in consequence, the Indians get along very nicely, albeit they are rather lazy, not to say slothful. They are poor fishermen and worst hunters, however, having for some reason lost the cunning of their ancestors.

Romances of the St. Clair River

"As precious as gems in a diadem
Are beautiful islands on the bosom of a noble river."

- Ellen Erg.

FROM TASHMOO PARK TO ALGONAC, on the left side lies Harsen's Island. It is well settled, and having been agricultural land ever since the country was inhabited by white men; beautiful Grande Pointe is on the upper end of the island. From Algonac clear to Port Huron, both sides of the river are in a good state of cultivation, for the soil is rich, yielding generous crops.

There are Indian mounds on Harsen's Island and Indian graves on all other islands in the river all the way to Port Huron. The first Harsen bought the island from the Indians, with the sanction of the British government. A Stewart moved in and set up a distillery, and then the Indians loved the spot more the ever. The Harsens died and the Stewarts died, but their "heirs and assigns" still live. There is a Harsen burial ground on the island in the very center of a grove of trees. Some of the graves are marked with cracked or broken slabs, bearing the names and dates of a past century. Over all is the growth of wild grave moss, once planted with loving hands: "and the sun glints down through thick foliage, tracing flickering shadows on the prostate tombstones."

The St. Clair River is as beautiful a stream of water as can be found in the world over. Only thirty-five miles long, and the dividing line between this part of the United States and Canada: it is broad and deep, with occasional bluff-like banks and along its shores alternate bustling cities and villages and primeval forests.

Fawn Island, opposite Marine City, which has the pioneer shipyards of the Great Lakes, is about a mile long and a half mile wide. It has a fine bathing beach. And upon its upper part is an Indian burying ground.

Further up the river is the Oakland, with its lawn and forest background, and then comes Stag Island, between St. Clair and Port Huron. The upper end of the island is wooded, the lower portion ends in marsh, the home of many kinds of wild fowl. A landscape artist has made Stag Island a beautiful park. On it many artistically designed cottages and a hotel has been erected. The tree lined roadways with their overhanging branches, and the sandy beach help to make it the ideal summer resort.

And so, traveling ever northward, The White Star Line sreamers finally reach Port Huron, " The Tunnel City" with its 35,000 to 40,000 inhabitants, its beautiful park, splendid public buildings, fine streets and good street car services.

Just beyond Gratiot, Huronia, and other beaches located directly on Lake Huron, and catching all the ozone laden breezes that blow. These are noted summer resorts and do a large profitable business.

Port Huron is called "The Tunnel City" because here the Great Trunk Railroad passes under the St. Clair River. The tunnel is some three miles long, and soon will be equipped with four mammoth electric locomotives that will haul trains back and forth. The tunnel will be provided with four hundred incandescent electric lights and all the iron work will be painted white to reflect the light and make this underground passage as light as day. This great engineering feat was completed in 1891 at a cost of $2,700,000. There is now being dug another tunnel connecting Canada with the United States, this time under the Detroit River at Detroit. It will be used by all the roads centering in Detroit, and will prevent the freight blockades that occasionally occur during severe winter weather, when the transfer boats are unable to push their way through the ice. Thus the uniqueness of the St. Clair and Detroit Rivers is under the water as well as above ground. They may not all be seen from a streamers deck, but the fact that they are there adds interest to the journey. Half the joys of life are in the imagination, anyway.

Opposite Port Huron is Sarnia. Ont. Where the White Star Lines steamers make direct connection with the Northern Navigation steamers for Sault Ste. Marie, Port Authur and Duluth, and the Grand Trunk Railway for Stratford, London, Hamilton. Toronto and all points in Canada.

Sarnia is a hustling little Canadian city of 12,000 inhabitants and growing rapidly. Here is located the largest oil refinery in the country, the product of which goes to supply all the provinces.

Just above the town, in the long sweep of Sarnia Bay, are the greatest saw mills of Western Canada. Great piles of lumber line the shore, and acres of uncut logs fill the bay, all of which have been rafted hundreds of miles down Lake Huron from the famous pine forests of the beautiful Georgian country. At the lower end of town is located the Canadian end of the Great International Tunnel, through which 360,000 cars annually pass under the river. Sarnia has numerous thriving and important industries, and at the present writing there is a reason to believe that the United States Steel Company contemplate the erection there of an immense steel plant. Just below the city limits, along the riverfront, is an Indian reservation similar to that on Walpole Island, the characteristics of which have been previously described.

Above the city at the foot of Lake Huron and reached by a pleasant ride on the Sarnia trolley cars, Lake Huron Park and Woodrow Beach is located.

Lake Huron is beautifully situated on rising ground with the waters of grand old Lake Huron in prefect view. The ever changing panorama of sail and steam ships coming and going over its broad bosom, which from day to day responds to the varying moods of nature, is a delight to the eye, changing as it does from the foaming whitecaps to a soft ripple or glassy smoothness, while the musical wash of the tiny waves on the shore soothes the nerves like a lullaby. The marvelously brilliant sunsets of Lake Huron are a glory of colors unequaled for beauty even on the far-famed Mediterranean.

Homeward Bound

"My mind's made up! No more afar I roam:
Now I will up and mend my way towards home."
-From Fact and Fancy

THE TRIP FROM PORT HURON TO DETROIT, southward, is more than a repetition. No one can see all the beauties of a landscape at the first glance. It must be visited at all hours of the day-morning, noon and night-when the sun is rising and when the sun is setting, when the shadows are first to the west and then to the east. So, it is with the trip between Detroit, Port Huron and Toledo. The viewpoints are not the same, the conditions are different. At evening the great salt works along the St. Clair look still larger. The Canadian towns of Sombra, Courtright, Port Lambton, and Sarnia take on new attractions; even the crowds idly watching the outgoing and incoming passengers do not appear the same. The personelle has changed, also the demeanor.

As the sun sinks to rest in the west, a peaceful quietness begins to settle down over the waters, and one by one twinkling lights appears. The rich coloring in the western sky fades into somber hues, and as the steamer rhythmically throbs its way through the water, the wake of foam and stray assumes regular undulations of black and white. The glories of the day are replaced by the beauties of the night, as a thousand stars bedeck the heavens with their twinkling spangles.

At the landing, dockmen swing their signal lanterns, and the crowds, weary with the day's pleasures, file on board and sink contentedly in the easy chairs liberally supplied. No one is compelled to stand; there are accommodations for all. The boats are never overcrowded, no one being allowed aboard when the legal limit of passengers is reached.

Before the Tashmoo nears the head of Belle Isle, and while passing between rows of buoys, the alternately red-and-white on Windmill Point-ten seconds white and four seconds red-and the Belle Isle light with its steady red glow, help to lay out the course the steamer will take. These are beautiful to watch, but more beautiful still are the tall towered electric lights of Detroit itself, every one of the two thousand candle power, casting their beams afar with unexcelled brilliancy and power. They appear to be in rows, the farthest ones hugging the horizon, while the lights from those near are brokenly reflected in the rippling waves of the Detroit River.

Even the vari-colored electrically lighted advertising signs along the river are worth considering. Advertising soaps or pills, stoves or whiskey, as they do, they are at least artistically designed, and tell in perpendicular, horizontal, and many angled rows of electric lights of business acumen.

The steamer blows a long whistle, and gracefully rounding to, reaches the White Star dock at 8:30. Two gangplanks are thrown out and in a few minutes all are ashore and on their way home.

> The day is done.
> The night lets down its sable robes,
> And merry throng, now silent,
> Seek their downy couches, and in their dreams,
> Live o'er the pleasures of the day.

A Word about the White Star Line Steamers

"These be the noble ships
And well worthy the designers fame."
-Anonymous

FOUR BOATS compose the fleet of White Star Line steamers. These are the Tashmoo, the Greyhound, the City of Toledo and the Owana, representing an investment of about a million dollars. All are speedy, and unexcelled in point of comfort and quality of service. In fact, the four boats combine a costly squadron of excursion steamers that it is impossible to match on fresh water. With three broad decks-hurricane, promenade, and main-there is ample room for sauntering couples, as well as quiet corners for those desiring the pleasure that comes from comfortable or secluded quarters.

The saloon on the promenade deck of the Tashmoo and Greyhound is a splendid example of how the public is accommodated by the White Star Line management. Wood work and furniture are solid mahogany, glistening with the finish of skilled hands and the touch of the designing artist.

Six handsome parlors are to be found on each side of the saloon, and each one is large enough to accommodate a dozen of persons. Here, with every convenience, including hot and cold water, passengers can gaze on the scenery through plate glass windows, or drawing the curtains, can find seclusion and comfort. They are rented to parties or individuals desiring privacy.

The dining room is on the main deck is finish in mahogany and marble, and surrounded by great windows of the finest imported glass, with china and silver service in harmony with the general elegance of the furnishings. The corps of stewards are men experience in catering to the public, and the best of food is furnished at the lowest possible price. The dining room, in fact, is not run for profit, but simply to furnish, at cost, meals to patrons of the line.

As the scenes change, or a landing is being made, passengers are apt to shift to the port or starboard side of the boat. To overcome this tendency to shift the center of gravity, there is a water ballast apparatus on each steamer, under the control of an engineer, who by simply moving a lever, shifts the ballast in harmony with the moving mass of living freight, thus keeping the hull on a even keel. The boats have steel hulls, collision bulkheads, and all other mechanical devices known to modern engineering which provide comfort and safety.

The following chapter, "Tashmoo, the Flagship of the White Star Line." Previously appeared in "Life at the Flats, the Golden Era of the St. Clair River Delta."

TASHMOO

THE FLAGSHIP OF
THE WHITE STAR LINE

The lingering memory of the Tashmoo name recalls the park and a special excursion steamer. In a by-gone era, excursion boating was a favorite form of recreation, readily available and modestly priced. The excursionist from Detroit could spend the day in Lake Erie or along the St. Clair River or arrange for a weekend or week-long cruise almost anywhere from the Straits of Mackinac to Niagera Falls. One could bask in the sun, promenade on deck under the stars dancing to the music of well-known bands. First class restaurants elegantly appointed and deckside picnic tables were available to cater to the varied dining interests.

The Tashmoo being loaded at her Detroit dock for a "Dodge Brothers" excursion to the Flats.

141

The Tashmoo was designed by Frank E. Kirby to be the speediest and most elegantly equipped day boat in the world. On Dec. 30, 1899, the next to the last day of the "Gay Nineties," the slender 300-foot hull was launched at the Wayandotte yards of the Detroit Shipbuilding Company. During, the winter the super structure was fitted with the finest appointments and on June 9, 1900, her inaugural run was made with great fanfare.

Launch of the Tashmoo's hull, December 31, 1899.

The exterior of the upper works were of pine, painted white to match the hull. The interior was finished in hardwood cabinetry. Quarter-sawed oak was used on the main deck, mahogany in the dining room and grand salon, and chestnut stained malicite was used in the smoking room.

One of the most memorable features of the Tashmoo was the plate-glass windows, so numerous and low that the passengers in the grand salon, dining room or smoking room could enjoy the scenery equally with those outside. Luxuriously furnished private parlors were provided with bay windows.

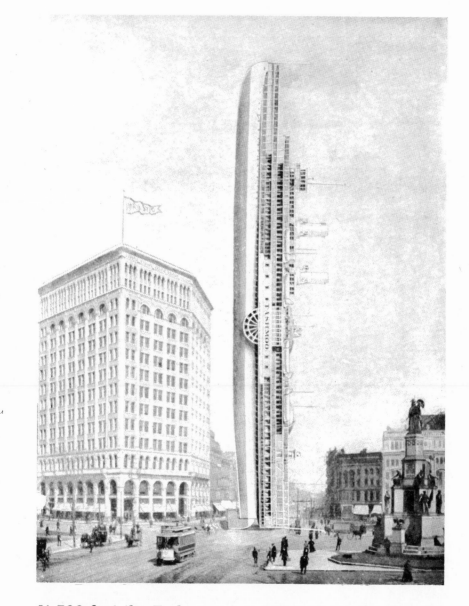

At 300 feet the Tashmoo was 109 feet greater than the
Majestic Building. The tallest building in Detroit in 1909.

President Theodore Roosevelt, upper left, was among the most prominent passengers to travel aboard the Tashmoo.

The Tashmoo entering the U.S. Ship Channel, above.

Arriving at the end of the line in Port Huron, below.

The social hall was covered with an elegant design of inlaid rubber tiling. The dining room and grand salon floors were covered with the best Wilton carpet that could be bought. Throughout, the furniture was nearly all mahogany.

The boat was designed to carry 4,000 passengers but she was limited to 2,800 to guarantee ample room. Every effort was made by the management to perfect and maintain the service of the new flagship at the highest possible standard.

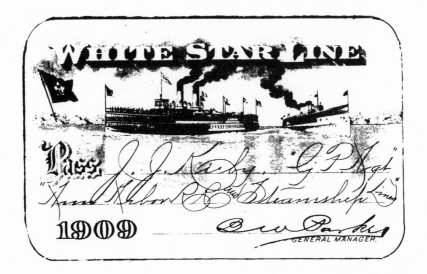

The Tashmoo offered wide shaded decks as well as the sun filled "C" deck. No view was obstructed thanks to the great expanse of glass. Over 600 windows offered a view unparalleled by any other steamer. Viewing her on a midnight cruise inspired the nickname the Glass Hack because all that could be seen from ashore were the hundreds of lights shining through the windows.

Over the years there were several changes made to the Tashmoo. After the first year her "C" deck was extended forward to the jackstaff and the pilot house was given a new roof line. In the 1920s, a large social room was added on the aft "C" deck and the officers' cabin was added aft of the pilot house on the hurricane deck. Over the winter of 1935-1936, sponsons were added for stability by increasing her beam to 43 feet. With the added weight of 100 tons, however, she was no longer capable of her legendary speed.

The rigorous schedule maintained by the Tahshmoo is well described by James Clary in "Ladies of the Lake:"

"During those early years, to say that the Tashmoo's schedule was a busy one was a gross understatement. In 1908 for example, ... leaving Detroit at 8:30 a.m., the ship would arrive in Port Huron five and a half hours and 20 stops later. Her longest stop, in St. Clair, was only 30 minutes while her briefest pause at Gus Trautz's Hotel near Harsens Island was an incredible three minutes. When upbound at the shorter stops, her big paddle wheels would continue to churn the water while she loaded scrambling, excited passengers. By 3:45 p.m., the Tashmoo would be slipping south from Port Huron, following her morning schedule in reverse and arriving back at her Griswold Street berth in Detroit by 8:30 p.m. on time! She maintained this almost unbelievable pace day after day, weekends included, during the summer months from the middle of June through September. Think of the maintenance efforts, the food replenishment, the fuel banking, the bookwork that made such a schedule possible. And there were no computers in those days."

Up to the very end there was never any intention but to maintain her in the finest condition. While her sponsons were being added to improve stability for the 1936 season, new furniture of chrome and leather were added in the dining room, the "C" deck beer garden was renovated and instead of a cleaning, her paintwork was given a new coating. For the last season she was as good as when first launched, and looked it.

Its Curse
Never did an excursion steamer enjoy a more glorious reputation. But the Tashmoo was a sidewheeler that bore an Indian name. Old-timers never stopped shaking their heads over that unfortunate combination. The old rivermen were persistent in predicting that the Tashmoo was bound to come to a bad end.

The story of the July 4, 1901, contest between the Tashmoo and the City of Erie is legend. The newer, faster Tashmoo was defeated by three boat lengths over a 95 1/2-mile course. Both ships continued to carry passengers for more than 30 years. (The City of Erie was moored and retired in Cleveland in the fall of 1937.)

As business continued to fall off in the 1920s the White Star Lines and its successors concentrated their resources on maintaining the 'Tashmoo. By the mid 1920s, the Sugar Island Park was sold and its rides moved to Tashmoo Park and all the steamers except the 'Tashmoo were sold.

For nearly 30 years the Tashmoo defied the skeptics but then on Dec. 8, 1927, in one of the worst storms ever on the river she was blown out of sight without a soul on board. The 60-mile-per-hour winds held back the waters from Lake St. Clair and the river's water level dropped over four feet. The strain was too great and the Tashmoo snapped her 14 heavy steel cables and she was blown up river. On the way, she smashed into the ferry Promise, which was building up steam for a run across the river. Upon impact, the crew of the Promise leaped to the dock.

147

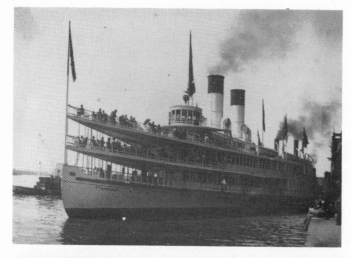

On her maiden voyage, June 9, 1900, the Tashmoo's "C" deck did not extend to the bow. The extension of the "C" deck was completed for the 1901 season. In the 1920s a large social room was added on the aft "C" deck, see page 153.

ON HER FIRST TRIP

Visibility was near zero and the Tashmoo seemed to disappear. She was heard banging against a concrete abutment of the Belle Isle Bridge. Listing tipsily to port with her sides gashed, she still seemed determined to bash her way through and up to Lake St. Clair. Tow tugs arrived and after a struggle to get lines aboard, they pulled the Tashmoo away from the bridge. Nearing her dockage she snapped the hawsers and once again plunged upstream toward the bridge. She was only 10 yards away from the bridge when the tugs subdued her once more. This time she followed them to harbor. Repaired and refurbished, she was ready for her first run the following season.

Seven years later, on Aug. 3, 1934, she was driven hard aground on the Canadian shore opposite Tashmoo Park. She was returning from Port Huron when a strong wind struck near Algonac. The captain decided to play it safe and stood offshore until the wind died down. Then just as they headed for the dock, the heaviest blow of the near hurricane struck. The 1,500 passengers were taken off in Coast Guard cutters and other small craft and waited at the park for several hours until the steamer Put-In-Bay could take them to Detroit. The Tashmoo, her paddle wheel smashed, was floated the next day.

On June 18, 1936, shortly after midnight while out for a moonlight charter, the Tashmoo struck a submerged rock. C.F Bielman, vice-president and general manager of the Tashmoo Transit Company, blamed the mishap on dredging operations that were being carried on by the government.

"We've been going down there for years," Bielman said, "and nothing happened. And now we go down on the same course and hit a rock ' "

The Tashmoo left her dock at 9:20 p.m. with a crowd of 1,400 gathered for the annual excursion of the Pals Club, a Hamtramck social group. She reached Sugar Island, near Grosse Ile, at 10:35 and started home at 11:20. As she came out of Sugar Island Channel, a shock was felt throughout the steamer. The impact put out the lights but most of the passengers did not know the danger until the Tashmoo was drawing up to the dock with the band still playing.

Before the last passenger was ashore, the Tashmoo was settling and within a few minutes the hull was resting on the bottom, the lower deck awash in 20 feet of water. The passengers, unperturbed built fires on the dock and sang songs while street cars were sent from Windsor and the Columbia was sent down from Detroit.
Safely back in Detroit, most of the passengers praised the Tashmoo's officers for keeping them unaware of the danger until the boat was docked. They also praised Jean Calloway and her orchestra for their coolness in playing uninterrupted after the crash and until the boat was safely docked. The last number as the Tashmoo settled into the river's bottom was "Old Man River."

Salvage attempts were begun almost immediately. Unfortunately, in their haste, the salvage crew raised one end too quickly and her keel was irreparably broken. That was the end of the Tashmoo's reign as "The Lady of the Lakes. "

The final blow to the Tashmoo did not take place until June 10, 1951. Since the Tashmoo was so beloved by thousands of excursionists, the dismantled parts of the vessel were auctioned. The pilot house and a large portion of the deck immediately below were purchased by Captain J. A. McKenty, a tugboat captain from Chatham.

Captain McKenty turned the cabin into a summer cottage at Mirwin's Park, near Chatham, Ontario, along the Chenal Ecarte

River. For many years the "Tashmoo Cottage" was an area tourist attraction. For many who had fond memories of the Tashmoo, it was a chance to view her once more.

Unfortunately, the curse of the skeptics continued. On June 10, 1951, the "Tashmoo Cottage" was completely destroyed by fire.

Largely through the efforts of Tashmoo historian J. Michael O'Brien, in May 1985 the Tashmoo was inducted into the National Maritime Hall of Fame at the U.S. Merchant Marine Academy in Kings Point, N.Y.

Views of the "B" deck salons when they were new with their fancy furnishings and Wilton carpets.

In later years much of
the Tashmoo's worn
carpeting was replaced
with linoleum.

Over the winter of 1935-1936 sponsors were added to the hull to comply with new government standards on stability. The domed room on C-deck was added in the 1920's

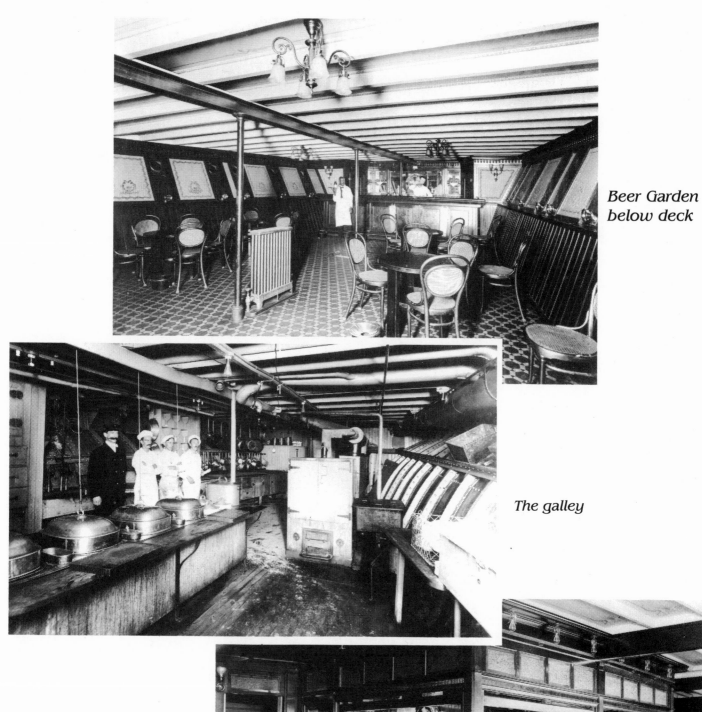

*Beer Garden
below deck*

The galley

*A refreshment stand
aboard the Tashmoo.*

154

Private rooms available on the Tashmoo

WHITE STAR ★ NAVIGATION CO.   ROOM CHECK   PASSENGER'S COUPON

Issued in exchange for Shore Office Ticket No._____or

	Punch cash paid on steamer.
STEAMER TASHMOO, ROOM NO. ____	$1.00
	2.00
From _____ To _____ ONE WAY	⌐.⌐0
BOUND TRIP	4.00
Good this date only _____ Aug 8 1925	5.00
Day Date	6.00
Passenger will retain this check as a receipt for amount of cash paid on Steamer or to show number of Shore Office ticket for which it was exchanged.	.25
THIS CHECK NOT VALID IF IT SHOWS ALTERATIONS OR ERASURES.	.⌐⌐
702 Form 29 General Passenger Agent.	.75

The furnishings of the Tashmoo were second to none. These views are of the ornate and spacious dining room.

On Dec. 8, 1927, in one of the worst storms ever to blow up the Detroit River, the Tashmoo blew out of sight in near zero visibility. Under the strain of 60 mile an hour winds, the Tashmoo snapped loose from her 14 heavy steel cables and started up river as if she was on her regular run up to the Flats. Before she could be located, she was heard banging against the Belle Isle Bridge. After breaking away from her rescuers once, the Tashmoo was finally subdued and brought back to her moorings. Repaired and refurbished, the Tashmoo was ready for her first run the following season.

On June 18, 1936, shortly after midnight, the Tashmoo struck a submerged rock. Salvage attempts were begun promptly. Unfortunately, in
their haste the keel was irreparably broken

The Tashmoo Cottage

The dismantled parts of the Tashmoo were auctioned. The pilot house was purchased by Captain McKenty from Chatham, Ontario. Captain McKenty's cottage became a landmark until June 10, 1951, when the Tashmoo cottage was destroyed by fire.

Pilot House & Main Salon of former S.S. TASHMOO now situated at Mirwin Park, Ontario, Canada

BLT-1902 — Columbia

Right,
STR. COLUMBIA
heading to Bob-Lo.
Note, Civic Center
dock and waiting
rooms at the foot
of Woodward.

Steamer Ste. Claire returning to Detroit

Bob-Lo Company — a Browning Line

Epilogue
THE STEAMER COLUMBIA
THE BOB-LO BOAT

The Steamers Columbia and Ste. Clair are still remembered by generations of area residents and guests. Beginning July 8, 1902, and May 7, 1910, respectively, and until September 2, 1991, these classic passenger steamers were dedicated to carrying excursionists from Detroit to Bob-Lo Island Amusement Park. Millions of passengers enjoyed cruises to the park, moonlight cruises into the lake and all-day trips as far as Port Huron.

The Columbia is the older of the two Bob-Lo boats, built in Wyandotte and Detroit in 1902 for the Detroit, Belle Isle & Windsor Ferry Company, owners of Bob-Lo. She is 216' long, 60' wide and 13'6"deep, below the waterline. She was last licensed to carry 2,500 people. Since November 2, 1992, she has been listed in the National Register and since July 6, 1992, she has been a National Historic Landmark, the highest status our government gives to historic resources.

The steamer Columbia and Ste. Clair, also a National Historic Landmark, are significant because they are the last classic excursion steamers in the country; because they are the last essentially unaltered ships designed by Frank E. Kirby; because they are the last surviving vessels of the Detroit, Belle Isle & Windsor Ferry Co.; and because they are among the few surviving vessels built by the Detroit Dry Dock Company. Columbia's 1,217-hp propulsion machinery survives almost intact from 1902, and is in operational condition. Notably, the Columbia is the oldest surviving passenger steamer in the United States. Restored, she would be the only operating ship of her type in the world.

THE STEAMER COLUMBIA FOUNDATION

Since the fall of 1991, the Columbia has been idle, her condition slowly declining. The following year she was designated as a National Historic Landmark. * Now, the Steamer Columbia Foundation, a 501 (c)(3) non-profit museum organization, has acquired the Columbia and intends to restore her for excursions on the Detroit River.

The first priority is to meet U.S. Coast Guard requirements so the Columbia can return to service. When that work has been accomplished, the ship can return to part-time active service for charters, excursions, and other events. The original plans will be used to restore the steamer to her 1902 condition, from a replica of her original tall black smokestack right down to the gilded moldings and hand-painted garlands of roses on the ceilings.

Initial funding has come from a low-interest loan from the National Trust for Historic Preservation, which has supported the project from its outset. Long-term funding will depend on popular support in the form of donations and volunteer assistance; government grant programs and corporate and foundation support.

Bob-Lo Island Amusement Park may be gone forever, but it may once again be possible to enjoy moonlight cruises or day trips to places like the St. Clair Flats. It may once again be possible to enjoy jazz and big-band events on her broad decks and big dance floor. Once again, we may be able to enjoy the cool breezes on a hot day watching scenes pass on Michigan's waterways as they can only be seen from a ship. We may again lean over the railing on the main deck to watch the historic triple-expansion steam engine as its connecting rods flash and its valve gear rocks to and fro. And all will be able to enjoy the sight of this classic steamer and listen again to the distinct steam whistle.

* National Historic Landmarks are nationally significant historic places designated by the Secretary of the Interior because they possess exceptional value or quality in illustrating or interpreting the heritage of the United States. Today, fewer than 2,500 historic places bear this national distinction. Working with citizens throughout the nation, the National Historic Landmarks Program draws upon the expertise of National Park Service staff who work to nominate new landmarks and provide assistance to existing landmarks. A friends group of owners and managers, the National Historic Landmark Stewards Association, also works to preserve, protect and promote National Historic Landmarks. (National Park Service, Internet: www.cr.nps.gov)

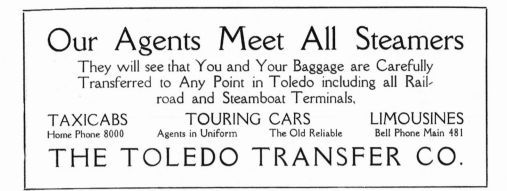

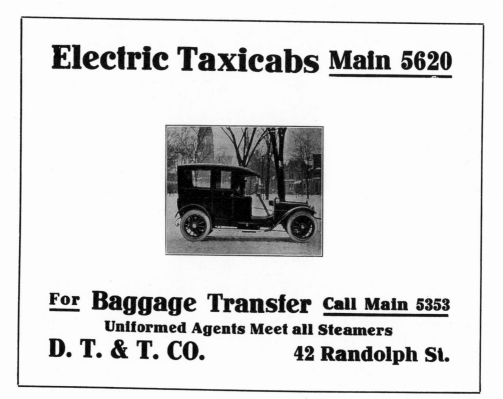

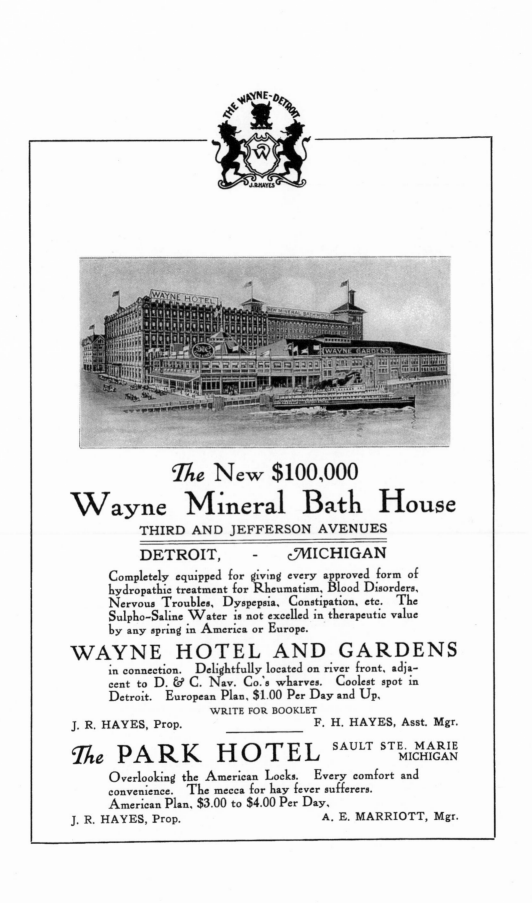

WHEN YOU ARE VISITING
DETROIT

TAKE ADVANTAGE OF THESE SIDE TRIPS

Steamers for **Belle Isle Park**

Every 20 minutes from foot of Woodward and Campau Aves., and from foot of Third Street. Fare, round trip, 10 cents.

Steamers for **Bois Blanc Park**

At 8.45 a. m. and 3.00 p. m., standard time, from foot of Bates Street. Returning at 1.30 p. m. and 8 p. m. Fare, round trip, 35 cts.

Steamers for **Windsor, Canada**

Every 10 minutes from foot of Woodward Avenue (three squares from D. & C. wharf). Fare, 5 cents.

BOIS BLANC PARK is on beautiful Bois Blanc Island situated at the mouth of the Detroit River. It is a perfect pleasure resort, the latest equipment, ample shelter for all kinds of weather, delightful music and modern Cafe. The large steel steamer **COLUMBIA,** having a capacity of 3500 passengers, is used exclusively in service on this route. Orchestra of 16 pieces furnishes the music on this new steamer. No liquors on the boats or at park.

Moonlights on the Columbia every Tuesday and Friday evenings at 8.30. Full orchestra. Fare, 35 cents.

Lake Ride on the Columbia Sunday evenings at 8.30. Concert music. Fare, 25 cts.

DETROIT, BELLE ISLE AND WINDSOR FERRY COMPANY

FRED. J. MASON,
GENERAL PASSENGER AGENT

WALTER E. CAMPBELL,
PRESIDENT AND GENERAL MANAGER

DO YOU KNOW

What a "Garland" Cabinet Gas Range Will Do for YOU?

No More Stooping—You stand erect, do all your baking or broiling in the natural, easy way. An Original "Garland" innovation.

You Broil and Bake Perfectly with the same set of burners—same heat; no excessive consumption of fuel. With the Glass Oven Door it is easy to get just the right brown without opening the oven door. Removable Parts and Smooth Castings are easy to keep clean.

And With All This—no hot kitchen, no fires to build, no fuel or ashes to carry, no muss, no dust; strike a match and it's all **at your service.**

There are **many more advantages** you can see for yourself at any of our one hundred local dealers or at the Gas Company's Office.

Gas Ranges in Every Type and Style

The
Michigan Stove Company
Largest Makers of Cooking and Heating Appliances
in the World

STOP IN AND SEE THEM

The J. L. Hudson Co.

GROWS WITH DETROIT

WOODWARD, GRATIOT
and FARMER

DETROIT, MICH,

✠

More than four hundred thousand feet of floor space—ten floors and a separate Basement Store—all devoted to the selling of good merchandise—the best that the markets produce.

✠

Quality plus Service—tells of the healthy growth of the House of Hudson.

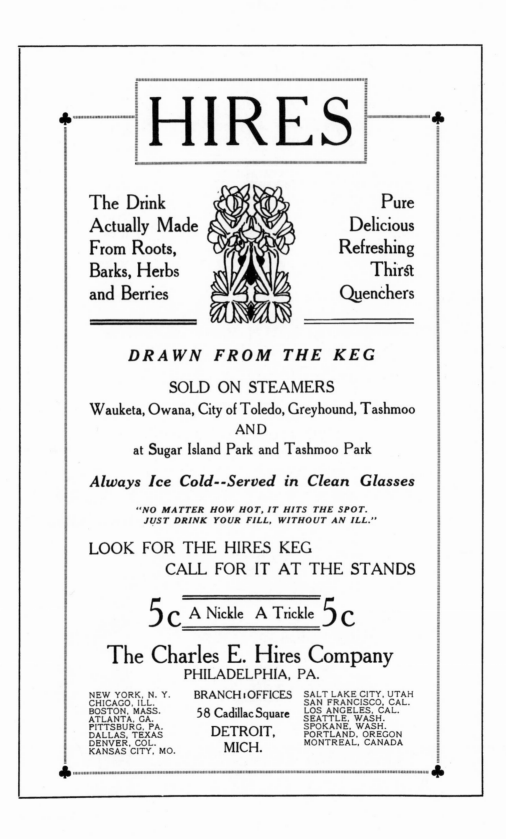

"The Spot for Hearty Appetite and Perfect Sleep"

The Star Island House

MICHIGAN'S FAMOUS SUMMER RESORT

REACHED BY WHITE STAR LINE STEAMERS

Star Island, St. Clair Flats, Mich.

ESTABLISHED 1878. 35 YEARS UNDER SAME MANAGEMENT

Star Island Particularly Appeals to Parties or Individuals Wishing to Spend Week-Ends Away from the City

Select Dancing Parties Every Evening

STAR ISLAND is in the Heart of the St. Clair Fishing Grounds, The Venice of America. Boats, Skilled Punters, Rods, Bait, and all necessaries for fishing. Sail boats, row boats, steam and gasoline launches. Bathing, bowling, lawn tennis, outdoor and aquatic sports. Large roomy verandas with lounging chairs, overlooking an ever-changing panorama of America's great merchant marine. More tonnage annually passes on the St. Clair River than passes any other point in the world, not even excepting the Suez Canal.

PRIVATE DINING ROOMS for SPECIAL PARTIES
LONG DISTANCE TELEPHONE CONNECTION

MRS. JAMES SLOCUM, Proprietor

1913—RATES FOR SEASON—1913

Breakfast 50c   Dinner and Supper 75c
Special Rates by the Week

SPECIAL ATTENTION GIVEN PRIVATE SUPPERS

Send for Illustrated Booklet, Care
White Star Line Steamers, Detroit, Mich.

Star Island House, Mich.

Watch for This Plant

View at St. Clair, Mich.

The Diamond Crystal Salt Plant at St. Clair

When you pass up or down the St. Clair, look for the home of the Diamond Crystal Salt Company.

Our plant is located in the southern part of the city. Watch for the mammoth electric sign and you cannot miss it.

Here's where "The Salt That's all Salt" and our famous Shaker Table Salt are made. The Diamond Crystal process of salt manufacture makes possible a product whose purity is attested by Government analysis. To those who stop at St. Clair we extend a cordial invitation to see how Diamond Crystal Salt is made.

Diamond Crystal Salt Co.
St. Clair, Mich.

STAG ISLAND
The Gem of the St. Clair River

THE GRIFFON STAG ISLAND   5429

The Most Complete Resort of the Great Lakes

Six miles from Port Huron and Sarnia, 55 miles from Detroit, Mich. Reached by White Star Line Steamers four times daily, also by interurban electric cars hourly from Detroit to Marysville, Mich., thence to island by our ferryboats.

Stag Island contains about 300 acres and is situated mid-stream in the St. Clair river between Detroit and Port Huron, Mich., and Sarnia, Ont., and within speaking distance of the greatest vessel traffic of the world—a moving panorama night and day.

A large natural forest of nearly 100 acres, vibrant with bird life, provides enchanting walks and shady nooks. The dancing pavilion, built entirely over running water, is one of the finest on the Great Lakes and the extensive verandas afford a charming marine view.

Excursions by land or water daily.

Rowboats, launches, lawn tennis, croquet, bowling, pool, bathing, baseball park and fishing.

This resort will appeal to ladies and children particularly, as no objectionable characters are allowed on the island.

Fish and chicken dinners for private parties and banquets arranged for if desired. Week ends a specialty.

Long distance telephone connections with all parts of the country.

Twenty-one completely furnished cottages, five to twelve rooms each, with toilets, running water, electric lights and sewer connections.

Two hotels with complete equipment. Hot and cold water.

For further information, rates, etc., address the manager of Stag Island, Marysville, Mich., or Corunna, Ont.

Hotel Harrington

Port Huron, Mich.

PORT HURON, easily accessible by water and rail from all points, is the most delightfully situated summer city on the great lakes.

THE HARRINGTON is one of the best furnished and equipped hotels in the middle west. Convenient, comfortable and satisfying, its appointments appeal alike to traveler and tourist.

AMERICAN PLAN $\left\{\begin{array}{l}\text{Rates \$2.50 to}\\ \text{\$4.00 Per Day}\end{array}\right.$

SPECIAL RATES BY THE WEEK

I. A. McDOUGALL, - - Manager

BIBLIOGRAPHY

Anderson, Janet, *Island in the City: Belle Isle, Detroit's Beautiful Island,* Companion book to an Exhibit at the Detroit Historical Museum, March 23-September 4, 2001.

Bugbee, Gordon Pritchard, a series of 22 laeflets donated bysome friends of the Dossin Great Lakes Museum and distributed on annual trips to Port Huron aboard the Bob-Lo boats.

Burdick, Jefferson R., The Handbook of Detroit Publishing Co. Post Cards, Syracuse, N.Y., 1954.

Burton, Clarence M., *The City of Detroit Michigan 1701-1922,* The S. J. Clarke Publishing Company, 1922.

Carlone, Chris, *Bob-Lo Island Amusement Park: The Story Continues,* uwindsor.ca/~carlone/boblo.html/ (website), last updated January 23, 1998.

Dixon, Michael M., *Life at the Flats: The Golden Era of the St. Clair River Delta,* Sterling Heights: Mervue Publications and St. Clair Delta Publishing, 1999.

Hyde, Charles K., *Detroit: An Industrial History Guide,* a publication of the Detroit Historical Society, circa 1985.

Hughes, Jim, *The Birth of a Century: Photographs by William Henry Jackson,* St. Martin's Press, New York, 1994.

Jackson, William Henry, *Time Exposure: The Autobiography of William Henry Jackson,* Tucson, Arizona, Patrice Press, Reprint Edition, 1994.

Kulisek, Larry, St. Lawrence Seaway, *Windsor Star,* December 2, 1999.

Prints and Photographs Division, Library of Congress. *Touring Turn of the Century America: Photography from the Detroit Publishing Co.,* memory.loc.gov/ammem/detroit/dethome.html, (website), last updated January 23, 2001.

Marquis, Albert Nelson, editor, *The Book of Detroiters*, Chicago, A. N. Marquis & Company, 1908.

Oxford, William, *The Ferry Steamers: The Story of the Detroit-Windsor Ferry Boats*, Toronto, Canada, Stoddart Publishing Co., Limited, 1992.

Read-Miller, Cynthia, editor, *Main Street U.S.A. in Early photographs: 113 Detroit Publishing Company Views*, Mineola, NY, Dover Publications, 1988.

Smith, Rockne P., *Our "Downriver" River: Nautical History and Tales of the Lower Detroit River*, Privately Published, 1997.

Schramm, Jack E., Henning, William H., Andrews, Richard R., *When Eastern Michigan Rode the Rails*, Interurban Press, 1984.

White Star Line Magazine, annual publications promoting summer cruises, 1906, 1911, 1913 and 1915

Woodford, Arthur M., editor, *Tonnancour: Life in Grosse Pointe and along the shores of Lake St. Clair*, 2 volumes, Detroit: Omnigraphics, Inc., 1994, 1997.

Appendix: Post Card Publishers

Following is the Publisher's information as found on the backs of the post cards, in the order they appear, beginning at the top of each page. Abbreviations and punctuation are unedited.

Page#
84. Published expressly for S.H. Knox & Co.
A.R.C.C. No. 246   7
A.R.C.C. No. 246   9

85. Pub. by Progressive News Co., Toledo, Ohio
Publ. by Edward M. Wright, Toledo, Ohio
   Printed in Germany

86. N/A
N/A

87. Pub. by Wolverine News Co., Detroit, Mich.   No. S22   Made in Germany
N/A

88. A.C. Dietche Detroit, Mich. and Leipzig   Made in Germany No. 560
Published by the Detroit and Windsor Ferry Co.
The Valentine & Sons Publishing Co., Ltd. Montreal and Toronto
   Printed in Great Britain.

89. N/A
N/A

90. N/A
"PHOSTINT" CARD. Made only by Detroit Publishing Company
VS- Superior Quality – Famous throughout the World

91. "PHOSTINT" CARD. Made only by Detroit Publishing Company
A. C. Bosselman & Co., New York.   Made in Germany   (Undivided Back)
PSC Co. Superior Quality

92. 530 Wolverine News Co., Detroit, Mich.   Printed in Germany
   (Double Card – Undivided Back)

93. (Both) Ralph Tuck & Sons' Post Card Series No. 2139, "Detroit Mich."
   Art Publishers to their Majesties the King and Queen
   (Undivided Backs)

94. N/A
Published by A. C. Dietsche, Detroit, Mich. and Frankfort, Germany.
   Made in Germany.

95. N/A
Made in USA

96. 19276
"PHOSTINT" CARD   Made only by Detroit Publishing Co.
   (Printed for Hiram Walker & Sons, Limited, Walkeville, Canada).

97. VS – Superior Quality - Famous Throughout the World.
Published by Wolverine News Co. Detroit, Mich.   Made in U.S.A.

98. CT Co. Chicago A-2717   (with description of the image on front).
A.C. Bosselman & Co., New York.   Made in Germany.

99. CT Co. Chicago R-27326   (with description of the image on front).
PSC Co. Superior Quality 1327 (with description of the image on front).

100. "PHOSTINT" CARD. Made only by Detroit Publishing Co.
The Valentine-Souvenir Co., New York.   Printed In U.S.A.

101. No. M 1910. Pub by The Detroit News Company. Detroit, Mich.
        AMERICHROME NANCY* Leipzig Berlin - New York-.
        Printed in the United States.
    No. 5437 Published by the Detroit News Company, Detroit, Mich. Leipzig, Dresden
        POLYCHROME NANCY* Germany
    A 7367 Published by The Detroit News Company, Detroit, Mich. Leipzig, Dresden
        Polychrome Nancy* Germany

102. DPC information on front only
"PHOSTINT" CARD   Made only by Detroit Publishing Co.

103. "PHOSTINT" Made only by Detroit Publishing Co.
"PHOSTINT" Made only by Detroit Publishing Co.
DPC information on front only

104. Published by Wolverine News Co., Detroit, Mich. and Leipzig, Germany.   No. 722.
        Made in Germany.
    N/A

105. Published by Wolverine News Co., Detroit, Mich. and Leipzig, Germany.   No. 728.
        Made in Germany
    DPC information on front only

106. No. C1078 Published by The Detroit News Company, Detroit, Mich.
        Dresden- Leipzig – Berlin   Made in Germany
        NANCY* LITHO-CHROME
    "PHOSTINT" CARD Made only by Detroit Publishing Co.

107. Published by Wolverine News Co., Detroit, Mich. and Leipzig, Germany   No. 726
        Made in Germany.
    "PHOSTINT" CARD Made only by Detroit Publishing Co.

108. The ROTOGRAPH Co. N.Y. City
"PHOSTINT" CARD Made only by Detroit Publishing Co.

109. Published by Wolverine News Co., Detroit, Mich. and Leipzig, Germany.   No. 732
        Made in Germany
        (Undivided Back)
    N/A

110. N/A   (Undivided Back)
"PHOSTINT" CARD Made only by Detroit Publishing Co.

111. The ROTOGRAPH Co. N.Y.City
      Printed in Germany
    Published by Wolverine News Co., Detroit, Mich. and Leipzig, Germany.   No. 731.
      Made in Germany

112. Published by Wolverine News Co., Detroit, Mich.   Made in U.S.A.
    Published by Wolverine News Co., Detroit, Mich. and Leipzig, Germany No. 716.
      Made in Germany

113. 259 Published by the Detroit News Company. Detroit, Mich.   Made in U.S.A.
    A 6101 Published by The Detroit News Company, Detroit, Mich., Leipzig, Dresden
    POLYCHROME NANCY* Germany

114. S-40 Wolverine News Co., Detroit, Mich.   Printed in Belgium.
    Published by Wolverine News Co., Detroit, Mich. and Leipzig, Germany No. 719.
      Made in Germany
    Pesha Photo Postcard Co.   Real Photo   Local Views   Marine City, Mich. U.S.A.

115. "PHOSTINT" CARD Made only by Detroit Publishing Co.
    S-43 Wolverine News Co., Detroit, Mich.   Printed in Belgium

116. (Undivided Back) N/A
    Pub. by J.J. Harper, Algonac, Mich.   Made in Germany   No. S439

117. No Publishing information but interesting details in the stamp box: Place the stamp here-
      ONE CENT- for United States and Island Possessions
      Cuba, Canada, and Mexico –TWO CENT- for foreign.
    No. 3 F.H. Holmes. Germany.

118. S-34 Wolverine News Co., Detroit, Mich.   Printed in Belgium
    Art Mfg. Co., Amelia, O.

119. Chas. H. Werner & Sons Co. Detroit, Mich.   Made in Germany
    DPC information on front only
    No. 2   Made in Germany

120. DPC information on front only — undivided back
    "PHOSTINT" CARD Made only by Detroit Publishing Co.
    N/A

*A three leaf clover bears the letters A, N, C in its leafs with the letter N printed on the left of the stem and the Y on the right.

N/A indicates that there is no identified publisher's mark available on the back side.

When Detroit Rode the Waves
Printing by Harlo Printing Company, 50 Victor, Detroit.
Type styles used: Benguiat Book BT eleven point on thirteen point leading.
with the exception of
"The Offerings of the White Star Line to a Recreation Seeking Public"
Caslon OldFace BT with Caslon Openface Heads.
Printed on 70 pound Finch Natural
Postcard section Potlach Mountie Matte 105 pound text
Cover 100 pound text Vintage Gloss

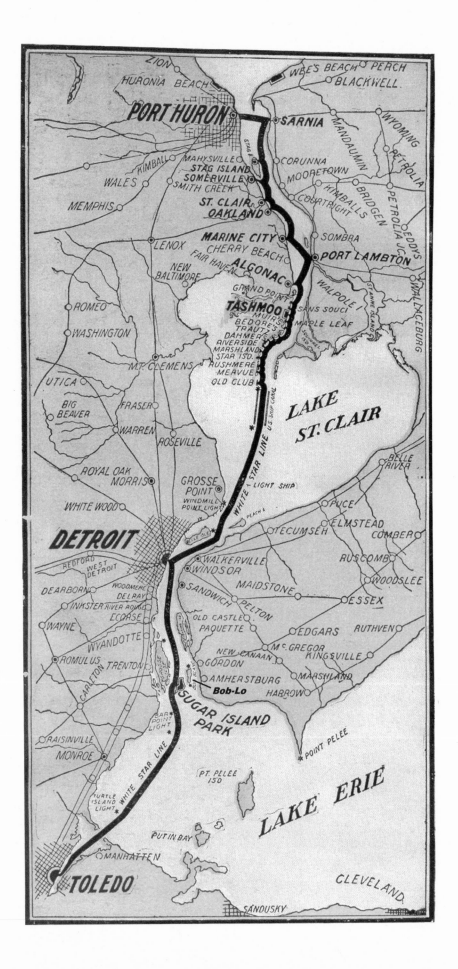